RELATIONALITY
From Attachment to Intersubjectivity

RELATIONAL PERSPECTIVES BOOK SERIES

STEPHEN A. MITCHELL AND LEWIS ARON
Series Editors

RELATIONALITY
From Attachment to Intersubjectivity

STEPHEN A. MITCHELL

THE ANALYTIC PRESS

2000   Hillsdale, NJ   London

Published by
The Analytic Press, Inc., Publishers
Editorial Offices:
101 West Street
Hillsdale, New Jersey 07642
www.analyticpress.com

Set in Book Antiqua and Zapf Humanist by
Christopher Jaworski (qualitext@earthlink.net)

Index by Leonard S. Rosenbaum

Library of Congress Cataloging-in-Publication Data

Mitchell, Stephen A., 1946–
Relationality : from attachment to intersubjectivity /
Stephen A. Mitchell.
p.   cm. — (Relational perspectives book series ; v.20)
Includes bibliographical references and index.
ISBN 0–88163–322–4
1. Object relations (Psychoanalysis). 2. Attachment behavior.
3. Intersubjectivity. 4. Psychoanalysis. 5. Psychotherapy. I. Series.

BF175.5.O24 M585 2000
150.19′5—dc21
00–033144

Printed in the United States of America
10 9 8 7 6 5 4 3 2 1

For Mannie Ghent

CONTENTS

PREFACE

Psychoanalysis has always been centrally concerned with human relatedness. The domain of psychopathology — psychoneurosis — which Freud wrested from the neurology of his day, was a realm in which mental events, rather than the purely physical, had become problematic, and the mental events Freud concerned himself with from early on had largely to do with relations with other people. In Freud's first theory, the early seduction theory, the toxic impact of the other, the seducer, was the causal force in the formation of psychopathology. That theory, in which the child was a blank slate, corrupted from outside, was too simple; the child's own wishes and longings, Freud came to feel, needed to be taken into account. In the abandonment of the seduction theory in favor of Freud's second theory, the instinct theory (in its various forms), the significant others became largely fantasied others, extrapolations from inborn drives. But Freudian drive theory always remained, necessarily, a *kind* of object relations theory, in which fantasies about others rather than the actions of others were crucial.

Similarly, the clinical process of psychoanalysis has always been fundamentally relational. Freud's self-analysis took place within the ambivalent intensity of his relationship with his friend Wilhelm Fliess. The peculiar structure of the analytic setting, a surrender to self-absorption in the presence of a very significant but largely quiet other, was shaped in no small measure by Freud's correspondence with his quasi-analyst. Letter writing, a largely lost art, provides for a particular kind of intense self-reflection in the context of addressing a very significant but nonintrusive other, who doesn't interact in the usual fashion.

So, even though relationality was salient in psychoanalysis from the very beginning, both in theory and in clinical practice, there were long stretches in the history of psychoanalytic ideas in which the nature of human relatedness was not studied and theorized about directly. As drive theory replaced the seduction theory as Freud's generative conceptual framework, the impact of events with real others, although never disappearing entirely, faded into the background. The content of the patient's mind was understood to derive from body-based, constitutionally wired primal fantasies, like oedipal triumphs, fratricidal murders, "primal scenes" of parental intercourse. Psychoanalysis became definitively *intra*psychic, and mental life was understood to arise in each individual, monadic mind, drawn only secondarily into relations with others. Other people were what Freud called "accidental" factors, attaining importance only through serendipitous linkage with drives. And the mother was understood to be, in the beginning, a "need-gratifying object," accruing psychical meaning only gradually through her function in reducing drive tensions. It is important to note that great advantages came from the abandonment of the overly simplistic seduction hypothesis. It opened the way for the extraordinary, unprecedented exploration psychoanalysis provided in the first half of the twentieth century into the subtle textures, conscious and unconscious, of human fantasy and imagination, but that journey into what was understood to be purely intrapsychic *did* leave relationality bracketed for many decades.

Similarly, in the psychoanalytic situation, the importance of the analyst as a significant other became partially occluded by Freud's establishment of the analyst as the authoritative interpreter of the patient's mental processes. The content of analytic sessions was understood solely as the expression of the intrapsychic material of the patient, with the analyst positioned outside that material, interpretively reading its deeper meanings. In recent decades, this classical vision of the analytic situation as comprised of one mind providing content for an interpreter has proved increasingly untenable. It is important to note that the scientistic properties of the classical analytic setup contributed to the establishment of psychoanalysis as the most disciplined and dedicated method ever devised for the study of human subjectivity; but, again, that methodology for the exploration into the workings of one mind did leave relationality, the intersubjective nature of the analytic situation, bracketed for many decades.

Why is the centrality of the relational so easy to miss, to forget about, to relegate to the conceptual background? It must have something to do with a confusion of minds with the ways in which bodies operate as functional units. Although human infants are dependent for many years on the physical care of adults, our bodily properties *seem* more or less prewired, unfolding in a maturational sequence[1] – from immobility to turning over, to pulling ourselves up, to crawling, to walking. Apart from severe pathology, we eventually attain an almost complete, physically functional autonomy. It is so easy to think of our minds in similar terms. We tend to take for granted an independent psychical existence in much the same way as we take for granted our independent physical existence. If I am living by myself, I must decide if I want to interact with others today; social interactions are intentional choices. And we tend to think of our minds similarly as our exclusive property, under our omnipotent control, with our intersubjective exchanges with others a product of our intentions. Thus, traditional theorists of motivation feel they have to supply us with reasons why people are drawn to each other: pleasure seeking, dependency, the need for security, sexual satisfaction, the desire for recognition, the division of labor, and so on.

These monadic, individualistic assumptions have been fundamental to Western culture over the past several hundred years and are taken for granted as part of ordinary experience. It is only relatively recently that they have been systematically called into question. Perhaps minds do not develop independently and secondarily seek each other out. Perhaps, as contemporary philosophers, linguists, and analytic theorists are suggesting, minds are fundamentally interconnected. Perhaps the question "Why am I hanging around with these other minded creatures?" is fundamentally misconceived, predicated on an inattention to a more basic interpenetrability of minds that makes individual mindedness possible in the first place.

Recent developments in the philosophy of mind provide a relevant parallel. Most historians of philosophy date the modern philosophical era at the point when Descartes dismantled and called into question everything he knew, in an attempt to anchor his understanding in certain knowledge. The only thing left standing after his radical skepticism had done its dirty work was doubt itself, leading him to proclaim, famously, "I think, therefore I exist." I'll start with my consciousness, which I can know for sure, Descartes reasoned, because this very doubting I am doing is an expression of it, and he then proceeded to rebuild his beliefs in the world around him, including other minds. Most contemporary philosophers tend to believe that Descartes made a wrong turn early on in his self-reflections. He took his thinking for granted, as a simple, basic, irreducible fact. We now believe that thinking, certainly the sort of thinking that Descartes involved himself in, is actually a complex achievement, not solely of an individual, but of a community, not any sort of community, but, specifically, a social, linguistic community. As Cavell (1993), drawing on Wittgenstein, Davidson, and others, has put it, "subjectivity arises along with intersubjectivity and is not the prior state . . . doubting the world and other minds, one must be in possession of all one needs to put the doubts to rest" (p. 40). Descartes did not have to derive the external world and other minds from his direct experience of his own mind; the very fact that he had a mind that could raise such questions presumed other minds and an external world they had in common. This is why solipsism, the belief that the only reality is one's own mind, even though a logical possibility, has never become a philosophical school. One mind *presumes* other minds.

Like Descartes, traditional theories of motivation, including the psychoanalytic and behavioral, begin with the individual organism, its physical needs, its interpersonal needs, its social needs. What are the various reasons we are drawn to each other? Picture an oak leaf on its branch asking "Why am I hanging around with these other leaves?" Motivational theory in psychology and psychoanalysis has taken for granted the individual nature of the psyche, in this case the oak leaf, and then provided motivations for object relations, or the fact that oak leaves tend to be found in clusters. But we are increasingly appreciating the implication of the fact that humans, like oak leaves, are not found in isolation, not possible in isolation. Human minds are fundamentally social phenomena that become focalized and secondarily elaborated by individuals.

There are some contemporary postmodern critics of object relations and attachment theories who argue that the relational turn in psychoanalysis, the establishment of relationality as a universal, fundamental feature of human development, is ethnocentric. Everything is culturally relative, the argument goes, including relationality and attachment. The fascinating thing about this critique of relational theory is that it takes for granted the very phenomenon it is critiquing. *Why* is everything culturally relative? It can only be because human beings are fundamentally, thoroughly cultural creatues. But why would culture be so important? It can only be because human beings *become* human beings through attachments to and internalizations of their caregivers and the particular culture they embody. Thus, the postmodern critique of relationality as universal and fundamental depends upon the presumption of relationality as universal and fundamental. We are so much embedded in our relations with others that those very relations are difficult to discern clearly. We are so in the thick of relationality that it is almost impossible to appreciate fully its contours and inner workings.

During the past several decades in psychoanalysis we have witnessed what might be considered a "relational turn," in which mind has increasingly been understood most fundamentally and directly in terms of self-other configurations, intrapsychically and interpersonally, present and past, in actuality and in fantasy. There are many different ways to characterize this broad, paradigmatic shift and many different areas of psychoanalytic thinking in which it has been quite evident.

In terms of theory building, there has been a gradual increase in the utilization of frameworks anchored in a variety of relational concepts for generating new ideas and organizing existing theory. Some continue to use the terminology of drive theory, but a closer look reveals that the meanings of the classical terms have changed. Freud's concept of "drive," perfectly consistent with the intellectual currents of his own time, was of an endogenous force of nature, pushing from within, that only secondarily comes into interaction with the external world. The most common concept of "drive" in the recent psychoanalytic literature is something quite different. Shaped by the highly influential metapsychological revisions of Loewald (1970) and Kernberg (1980), "drive" now generally indicates a body-based sexual or aggressive motive that has derived from, and has been shaped by, dense affective interactions with early caregivers. Drives, as Loewald (1970) put it, have a "relational character" (p. 292).

Other authors and clinicians have come simply to add relational principles to their repertoire, rather than to relationalize the concept of drive itself. Thus, many analysts (e.g., Pine, 1990) feel quite comfortable with a loose eclecticism, in which drive, object relations, interpersonal, ego, and self-psychological principles all coexist and are called into service by the clinical problem that emerges.

Within the major theoretical schools of analytic thought, there has been a distinct turn toward relational concepts. Contemporary Kleinian theory has been dominated by increasingly interactional versions of the concept of "projective identification," which has dramatically reshaped the Kleinian vision from a purely intrapsychic model of self-contained primitive phantasies to a dense account of complex reciprocal projective and introjective influences (see Spillius, 1988). Contemporary self psychology has become, in major respects, increasingly relational, particularly under the influence of intersubjectivity theory as developed by Stolorow and his collaborators. Many contemporary interpersonal analysts have moved in a relational direction, adding object relations concepts concerning internal object relations to the traditionally interpersonal account of actual transactions between people. And psychoanalytic developmental theory, across the board, has been greatly influenced by the impressive tradition of attachment theory (Goldberg, Muir, and Kerr, 1995), derived from John Bowlby's work and extended by Mary Ainsworth and Mary Main (1995), as well as by the richly relational, systems-theory methodology employed by infant researchers (Stern et al., 1998; Sander, in press) in studying the interactive field between children and caregivers.

In the theory of clinical technique too, relational concepts have been increasingly in evidence. The traditional classical principles of neutrality, abstinence, and anonymity, fashioned to protect the integrity of the patient as a monadic, one-person system, have generally been either abandoned or else revised into milder, less impersonal forms, emphasizing the "containing," "holding" features of the patient-analyst field. The terms "interaction," "intersubjective," and "enactment" have become virtual buzz-words that pervade the analytic literature, from the most established, traditional journals to the most recent and innovative. And the study of the array of patient-analyst interactions, linked variably with the terms "countertransference," "enactment," and "projective identification," has become, perhaps, the dominant focus of recent articles and books on analytic technique.

Thus, the relationality of mind has been explored both within and outside the analytic situation in many different ways. There is considerable confusion, however, about the relationships among these different interactional concepts and lines of thought: What do they have to do with each other? Are different theories of intersubjectivity (e.g., Trevarthen and Hubley, 1978; Stolorow, Brandchaft, and Atwood, 1987; Benjamin, 1988, 1998; Stolorow and Atwood, 1992) describing the same basic phenomenon in different terms, or do they concern themselves with different phenomena? (See Aron, 1996, chapter 2, on this question.) Does the term "intersubjective" have the same meaning as the term "interpersonal" (Sullivan, 1953; Lionells, et al., 1995)? What is the relationship between Loewald's object relations theory and Fairbairn's, or Bowlby's theory of attachment and recent explorations of intersubjectivity? Are the patterns of reciprocal influence depicted in the systems theory of infant researchers the same as self and ego representations of the ego psychologists? Different relational concepts seem to imply different kinds of boundaries between self and other, some more permeable (e.g., in Bion-based accounts of projective identification) and others struggling hard to emphasize the separation between the inner world of the patient and the inner world of the analyst (e.g., Jacobs, 1991). Are these different approaches predicated on alternative, competing theories about the nature of mind, or are they referring to different dimensions of human interaction? These concepts all suggest what Aron (1996) has termed a "mutuality" in the interaction between participants, but, as Aron has noted, there are many different forms of mutuality.

To address these issues in anything approaching comprehensiveness is clearly beyond the scope of a single book. The purpose of this volume is to point to the importance of such concerns and to suggest an approach to them. The framework I employ is based upon the premise that human minds interact with each other in many different ways, and that the variety of relational concepts pervading the recent analytic literature is best understood not as representing competing theories, but as addressing themselves to different, interwoven dimensions of relationality.

Part I presents a close reading of some of the major themes in the contributions of Hans Loewald. I start with Loewald because I find his vision of mind, subjectivity, and intersubjectivity extremely broad and rich. The central presupposition of Loewald's approach is that mind is a fundamentally temporal phenomenon, constructed according to varying organizational principles at different points in time. I want to use this basic Loewaldian approach to generate a framework to house some of the most important facets of relationality developed in the analytic literature of recent decades.

Loewald's work is difficult for most readers, not immediately accessible. On one hand, his writings consist of individual papers, fragments, written over the course of more than 20 years and never really knit together into a book or comprehensive theory; on the other hand, there is an extraordinary consistency to Loewald's work, recurrent themes that surface again and again in all his writings. In one respect, the language Loewald uses to introduce his thinking is the language of classical psychoanalysis in all its arcane, metapsychological density; in another respect, Loewald radically changes the meanings of all of the classical terms, so they come to mean something quite different than what Freud and his contemporaries had in mind. In one sense, Loewald is an extremely systematic thinker and writer, working his way through dense conceptual problems with intense attention to details; in another sense, there is a visionary quality to Loewald's thought, at times approaching a kind of mysticism, that breaks through in occasional passages of lyrical power. All this has made it difficult to locate Loewald either in the history of psychoanalytic ideas or within the contemporary landscape of diverse psychoanalytic perspectives. He is one of the most frequently cited authors within the current Freudian mainstream literature, but those who cite him rarely seem to appreciate the extent to which the radical nature of Loewald's thought challenges the very channel through which that mainstream flows.[2] And he is cited only occasionally (although increasingly) by postclassical or relational authors, who, misled by his use of traditional terminology, fail to notice that Loewald was struggling with many of the same issues that now dominate the writings of our most innovative contemporary authors, for whom his work might serve as a rich treasure trove of new ideas and inspiration.

Part II draws on some of the basic features of Loewald's vision to elaborate a framework for containing and contrasting basic relational concepts, like attachment, systems-theory, projective identification, object relations, and intersubjectivity. In chapter 3, I present four dimensions of interactional organization and two vignettes illustrating the ways in which they operate and intersect. In chapter 4, I explore the historical split and the current convergence between Bowlby's attachment theory and psychoanalysis. Using an extended clinical vignette, I suggest ways in which current relational concepts fill out the interior, intrapsychic processes through which Bowlby's more behavioral, ethological account of attachment operates. In chapter 5 I consider Fairbairn's revolutionary theory of object relations, for decades a powerful presence in the background of analytic thought, recently emerging into the foreground and cited by many contemporary authors. One way in which Fairbairn's work has been recently embraced is through hybrid or mixed models, in which Fairbairn's emphasis on object-seeking is combined with Freud's emphasis on pleasure-seeking. I argue that such a use of Fairbairn actually obliterates the major significance of his contribution; I further demonstrate how integrating Fairbairn's work with other relational perspectives provides a compelling alternative framework for understanding phenomena like powerful sexual and aggressive impulses and guilt, most often associated with (pleasure-seeking) drive theory. Finally, in chapter 6 I use the synthetic relational framework developed in the previous chapters to consider the intensely intersubjective nature of clinical work and the center of many of the current controversies in analytic technique: the tensions between expressiveness and restraint in the analytic relationship.

ACKNOWLEDGMENTS

I am grateful to many friends and colleagues for reading parts or, in some cases, all of various versions of this book and giving me very useful feedback. They include: Neil Altman, Lewis Aron, Tony Bass, Jessica Benjamin, Margaret Black, Phil Bromberg, Peggy Crastnopol, Jody Davies, Muriel Dimen, Mannie Ghent, Adrienne Harris, John Kerr, Karen Maroda, Susie Orbach, Michele Price, and Paul Stepansky.

An earlier version of chapter 1 was presented at the Toronto Institute for Contemporary Psychoanalysis on September 20, 1997, and at the Horney Institute in New York on December 11, 1997, and was published in *Psychoanalytic Dialogues* (8:825–855). An earlier version of chapter 2 was presented at the New School for Social Research conference "From Ghosts to Ancestors" on March 26, 1999. An earlier version of chapter 3 was presented at the Manhattan Institute of Psychoanalysis on February 28, 2000. An earlier version of chapter 4 was presented as the annual John Bowlby Memorial Lecture at the Center for Attachment-Based Psychoanalytic Psychotherapy in London on February 14, 1998, and at the Association of German Psychoanalytic Institutes in Lindau, Germany, on September 25, 1998, and was published in *Psychoanalytic Dialogues* (9:85–107). An earlier version of chapter 5 was presented at the Fairbairn conference in New York City and was published in *Fairbairn, Then and Now* (1998, The Analytic Press), edited by Neil Skolnick and David Scharff. An earlier version of chapter 6 was presented at the Massachusetts Institute for Psychoanalysis conference "Love and Hate in the Analytic Relationship" in Boston on October 17, 1998, and at the Israeli Psychoanalytic Society on February 29, 2000.

RELATIONALITY
From Attachment to Intersubjectivity

RELATIONAL PERSPECTIVES BOOK SERIES

Volume 20

PART I

FROM GHOSTS TO ANCESTORS
The Psychoanalytic Vision Of
Hans Loewald

CHAPTER 1

LANGUAGE AND REALITY

Cosmologists tell us that our universe began in a primal density in which all the structures and differentiations we take for granted were collapsed in on one another. The constituents of future atoms and molecules were all there, but they were packed together tightly. Our world, the world as we know it, has evolved into atoms and molecules, stars and galaxies, and planets, animals and people, and spaces, vast spaces. The explosive force that powered all that development into differentiated and bounded entities is called the "Big Bang." But perhaps the greatest mystery of modern astronomy is that the extraordinary centrifugal rush into differentiated structures and boundaries and spaces seems to be balanced by an opposite, centripetal force that keeps all those structures from flying apart, that brakes the force of the Big Bang, that connects the seemingly separate and autonomous elements of our universe, and that may eventually draw them all back together again into yet another cataclysmic rebirth. There is something else, "hidden matter" in the seeming vacancy of all that space, that generates enough gravity to tie together even galaxies rushing apart across mind-numbing distances into a single force field.

Perhaps it is not too fanciful to think of psychoanalysts as astronomers and cosmologists of the mind. Patients begin treatment with fragments, pieces of a life that seem bounded and separate from one another: symptoms, current "reality" problems, memories, dreams, and fantasies. Psychoanalysts have learned to think of these seemingly bounded fragments in psychic space as constituents of a single force field. And psychoanalysts, together with their patients, narrate not cosmologies, but developmental histories in which they speculate about the way that the force field of the patient's life came to be.

Hans Loewald developed a psychoanalytic vision of the nature and origins of mind, a vision of extraordinary richness and explanatory power. Like contemporary cosmology, it begins with a primal density in which all of the features of our everyday world, which we take to be separate, bounded elements, are collapsed in on one another. We begin, Loewald suggests, with experience in which there is no differentiation between inside and outside, self and other, actuality and fantasy, past and present. All these dichotomies, which we come to think of as givens, as basic features of the way the world simply is, are for Loewald complex constructions. They arise slowly over the course of our early years and operate as an overlay, a parallel mode of organizing experience that accompanies and coexists with experiences generated by the original, primal unity.[1] That earliest form of experience, Loewald suggests, never disappears. It underlies the later differentiations and bounded structures that make adult life possible. That original and continuing primal density, in Loewald's vision of mind, operates as "hidden matter," tying together dimensions of experience that only appear to be fully separate, bounded, and disconnected. In fact, in Loewald's view, psychopathology most broadly conceived represents an imbalance between the centrifugal and centripetal forces of mind. In psychosis, the primal density undermines the capacity to make adaptive, normative distinctions between inside and outside, self and other, actuality and fantasy, past and present. In neurosis or, Loewald occasionally suggests, the normative adaptation to our scientistic, hypertechnologized world, the constituents of mind have drifted too far from their original dense unity: inside and outside become separate, impermeable domains; self and other are experienced in isolation from each other; actuality is disconnected from fantasy; and the past has become remote from a shallow, passionless present.

The story of Loewald's own earliest years (Elizabeth Loewald, personal communication) may serve as the best introduction to his vision of the original dense unity into which we are all born. Hans Loewald was born into his mother's grief. His father died shortly after Hans's birth, and thus he drew his first breaths in a world suffused with his mother's mourning and the powerful presence of his father's absence. She was a pianist of considerable skill and, as she told him later, consoled herself in the months following the death of her husband by playing Beethoven's piano sonatas, often with Hans in his crib placed carefully beside the piano stool. Think of the transformative affective power of the "Moonlight" and "Appassionata" sonatas, and then try to imagine the experience of that baby. How could he possibly separate his own feelings from his mother's, his father from Beethoven, an inner world of his own generation from an outer world filled with loss and passion, a past when his father was present from a present from which his father had passed? Perhaps the emotional intensity and drama of Hans Loewald's early months had something to do with the importance he placed on a primal dense unity as the starting point for the psychic universe that constitutes each individual human mind.

LANGUAGE

Because Loewald understood every dimension of experience as proceeding from the original primal density, any of the major topics Loewald concerned himself with — drives and objects, fantasy and reality, time, memory, and mourning, internalization and sublimation — can be traced back to its entanglements with the others. One *could* begin anywhere. Yet, somehow it seems most appropriate to ground an initial approach to Loewald's thought in a consideration of his understanding of language, because he was so mindful (for reasons that I make clear later) of the language in which he chose to present his ideas.

Most philosophers and psychologists of language regard early human development as bifurcated by a fundamental and perhaps unbridgeable divide between the preverbal and the verbal. Increasingly over the course of the 20th century, language has become understood as the material out of which adult mentation is generated, the very stuff of mind. Following Wittgenstein and Ryle, thinking is often discussed as interiorized speech; following Lacan, many understand the unconscious itself in terms of linguistic structures. A divide has opened up between the early months of life, before the child is inducted into the linguistic-semiotic system through which he will become a person, and his later psychological self.

Psychoanalytic theorists of language, depending on their own sensibilities, have different attitudes toward life on either side of the chasm (Cavell, 1993, following Wittgenstein, calls it the "veil of language") between the preverbal and the verbal. For Sullivan (1950), who valued the precision of language above all else, the movement from the preverbal to the verbal represents the emergence of the distinctively human from the animal.

> Don't permit yourself to think that the animal can be discovered after it has been modified by the incorporation of culture: it is no longer there. It is not a business of a social personality being pinned on or spread over a human animal. It is an initially animal human developing into what the term human properly applies to—a person. . . . While the many aspects of the physio-chemical world are necessary environment for every animal—oxygen being one—culture, social organization, such things as language, formulated ideas, and so on, are an indispensable and equally absolutely necessary part of the environment of the human being, of the person [pp. 210–211].

On the other hand, for Daniel Stern (1985), who is fascinated with the cross-modal sensory textures and affective richness of early experience, the advent of language is a mixed blessing. In its communicative function, language makes possible the generation of what Stern terms "the sense of a verbal self," making many features of our experience now knowable and shareable, opening up "a new domain of relatedness" (p. 162). Yet, whereas Sullivan sheds no tears over what is lost when the "veil of language" renders inaccessible what has gone before, Stern regards the advent of language as a

> double-edged sword. It also makes some parts of our experience less shareable with ourselves and with others. It drives a wedge between two simultaneous forms of interpersonal experience: as it is lived and as it is verbally represented.[2] Experience in the domains of emergent, core- and intersubjective relatedness, which continue irrespective of language, can be embraced only very partially in the domain of verbal relatedness. And to the extent that events in the domain of verbal relatedness are held to be what has really happened, experiences in these other domains suffer an alienation. (They can become the nether domains of experience.) Language, then, causes a split in the

experience of the self. It also moves relatedness onto the impersonal, abstract level intrinsic to language and away from the
personal, immediate level intrinsic to the other domains of
relatedness [pp. 162–163].

Stern and Sullivan have quite opposite sensibilities. When words
first appear, Sullivan suggests, they embody the particularities of
their original context. Thus, when the baby says "ma-ma," everyone
gets very excited. But these "parataxic" features, Sullivan believes,
are usefully lost as language use takes on "consensual validity" and
moves into the domain that he terms the "syntaxic." The abstract
nature of language strips words of the idiosyncratic features of their
first appearance, and this is all to the good. Language can now be
used in a way that other speakers can understand precisely, and the
residues of the original parataxic contexts remain as autistic pockets
that detract from and compromise potentials. Humanity, Sullivan
believes, takes place in interpersonal interaction. For Stern, on the
other hand, the richest forms of experience emerge in the preverbal
realm, with its densely sensual, cross-model textures. This sensual
intensity is lost with the advent of language. Like Sullivan, Stern
seems to regard the loss as inevitable; unlike Sullivan, Stern regards
the loss as tragic, a poignant compromise that inevitably accompanies development into social interaction.

Freud also made a sharp distinction between the preverbal and
verbal realms. Language is associated with secondary process, the
reality principle, the "word-presentation," the present-day adult
world and is at considerable remove from the "thing-presentation,"
the preverbal, fantasy-driven workings of primary process. In fact,
consciousness itself is linguistically coded. In order for the unconscious, infantile impulse that generates the motive force of a dream
to enter awareness, it has to piggyback onto words provided by the
residue of the present day's experience. Thus Freud too saw a gulf
between the preverbal and verbal domains.

The key feature of Loewald's understanding of language is his
challenge of that separation.[3] For Loewald, language transcends the
distinction between preverbal and verbal; language begins to play an
important role in the earliest days of life. The most important distinction is not between preverbal and verbal, or between primary and

secondary process, but between the *ways* in which language operates in these two developmental eras and levels of mental organization.

In the beginning, Loewald (1977a) suggests, language is a key feature of an original "primordial density" (p. 186) in which feelings, perceptions, others, self are all part of a seamless unity.

> She [the mother] speaks with or to the infant, not with the expectation that he will grasp the words, but as if speaking to herself with the infant included . . . he is immersed, embedded in a flow of speech that is part and parcel of a global experience within the mother–child field [p. 185]. While the mother utters words, the infant does not perceive words but is bathed in sound, rhythm, etc., as accentuating ingredients of a uniform experience [p. 187].

Loewald is suggesting that the very distinction between preverbal and verbal developmental epochs is misleading, that there is no preverbal domain per se. Rather, language is an intrinsic dimension of human experience from birth onward. The meaningful distinction is between a developmental era when words, as sound, are embedded in a global, dense undifferentiated experience, and a later era, when the semantic features of language have taken precedence over its sensual, affective features. In his retooling of Freud's own language, Loewald characterizes the significant divide as a distinction between language *in* primary process and language *in* secondary process.

Some recent findings of infant researchers (DeCasper and Fifer, 1980) illustrate Loewald's point. Pregnant women, during the last trimester, read aloud the Dr. Seuss classic *The Cat in the Hat* to their fetuses. Shortly after birth, the babies preferred a tape-recording of their mother's voice reading that story to hearing her read another Dr. Seuss story. As Beebe, Lachmann, and Jaffe (1997) note, these babies are clearly able to "distinguish slight differences in rhythmicity, intonation, frequency variation, and phonetic components of speech" (p. 137). Consider this astounding finding for a moment. Words are a salient feature of babies' experience, not only *after* birth but in utero. Babies distinguish remarkably subtle features of spoken words (after all, they tested two different Dr. Seuss stories, not Dr. Seuss and Hegel). Perhaps most important for Loewald, the earliest experience of language is deeply embedded and embodied in the child's undifferentiated union with the mother inside of whom he slowly grows into awareness.[4] In the beginning, the word, the body, affect, relational connection—these are all indistinguishable components of a unified experience.

Gradually, over the first several years of life, language takes on a very, very different quality. The child slowly comes to understand the abstract, semantic significance of words; words have meanings, apart from the immediate sensory, affective context in which they appear. Language takes on an increasingly denotative significance, and language skills entail the ability to use words in a way that anyone, not just mother, can understand, words that have, in Sullivan's terms, a syntaxic, consensual validity.

Thus Loewald suggests that, over the course of early development, language comes to function in a secondary-process mode rather than in a primary-process mode, facilitating an adaptive competence in dealing rationally with everyday reality.

What happens to the primary-process experience of language after language has become harnessed for secondary process purposes? This question of the fate of earlier modes of organization is always the central issue for Loewald, in every major psychodynamic dimension, in assessing the quality of psychic life. And for Loewald, balance is always the crucial concern. On one hand, if linkage does not become abstracted, sufficiently broadened from its original primary-process context, the child remains entangled in a dysfunctional, incompletely differentiated autistic state. On the other hand, if language has been drawn too completely into secondary-process functions, if the original affective density of language has been almost completely severed, the result is a functionally competent but affectively dead and empty life.

There is a deep link between the same words in their primary-process and secondary-process forms. The key question for Loewald is: How alive is that link? Does language in its adaptive, everyday (secondary-process) form resonate with its earlier sensory, affective, undifferentiated (primary-process) origin, or has a severing split the two realms from each other? Such a delinking becomes definitive of Loewald's reworking of Freud's concept of "repression," no longer the denial of access to awareness for an impulse, fantasy, or memory, but a severing of developmentally earlier from later forms of experience and psychic organization.

An experience with my younger daughter brought these issues home to me in a powerful way.* She was one year old, beginning to use words in an enthusiastic fashion, which was very exciting to me. We would sit at the breakfast table, and she would hold her little cup up to me, saying emphatically something like "Numa numa numa numa jooooose." I would respond by looking her intently in the eye and saying back, pronouncing the words slowly and very distinctly, something like "Samantha, would you like some more juice?"

Now it just so happened that I was reading Loewald's "Primary Process, Secondary Process and Language" (1977a) around this time, and I began to reflect on how I was responding to my daughter. I seemed to have the idea that I was doing her a favor by helping her shape her babyish, playful way of asking for more juice (or at least that is what I assumed she was doing) into words that any English-speaking interlocutor could recognize and respond to. But, reading Loewald made me notice how much more fun her way of using language was than mine, how much was lost in this lesson in linguistic competence I was offering her. I began to fear that I might, in fact, be ruining her life. She might become very competent at requesting drinks, but lose the vitality and sensuous playfulness that helped make her so delightful. So, rather than teaching her to talk the way I did, I began to mimic her way of talking. The experience was much more fun, more engaging, sensuously rich. I did have occasional moments when I pictured her in a college cafeteria line, humiliating herself by asking for a drink in the same way. Over time, of course, she managed to learn to speak in a normative fashion. But Loewald's hope would be that there would remain a vital link between her adult experience of drinking and asking for more and her earlier affectively and sensuously laden experiences. It is language that provides that life-enriching link between past and present, body and world, fantasy and reality, and language is deeply embedded in its original relational context: "The emotional relationship to the person from whom the word is learned plays a significant, in fact, crucial part in how alive the link between thing and word turns out to be" (Loewald, 1977a, p. 197).

---

*I used this anecdote previously (Mitchell and Black, 1995) to illustrate Loewald's theory for a nonprofessional readership.

In the following passage, embedded in the middle of dense meta-psychological language, Loewald (1977a) gives us a glimpse of his vision of life, with the richest, most vital forms of experience halfway on a continuum with psychotic chaos on one end and schizoid hyperrationality on the other.

> In everyday mental functioning repression is always more or less at work; there is a relative isolation of word(s). . . . Indirect . . . or weak links usually remain, sustaining an average level of mental functioning that represents a viable compromise between too intimate and intense closeness to the unconscious with its threatening creative-destructive potentialities, and deadening insulation from the unconscious where human life and language are no longer vibrant and warmed by its fire. This relative deficiency or weakness of links between verbal thought and its primordial referents makes it feasible for language to function as a vehicle for everyday rational thought and action, comparatively unaffected by or sheltered from the powers of the unconscious that tend to consume rationality [pp. 188–189].

Note the subtle but crucial shift in metaphors regarding the unconscious here, from Freud's "seething cauldron" to a hearth. The salient feature of the unconscious for Loewald is not explosive energy or propulsive drives, but rather its dedifferentiating impact. Alongside differentiated, adaptive, secondary-process experience is an earlier primordial organization of experience of dedifferentiation, affective density, and fusion. The key determinant of the quality of experience is the relation between these two realms (sometimes Loewald talks of them as "levels of organization"). Repression severs the connections or links between them; language has the capacity to bridge them. Language, Loewald (1977a) suggests, "in its most genuine and autonomous function is a binding power. It ties together human beings and self and object world, and it binds abstract thought with the bodily concreteness and power of life. In the word primary and secondary process are reconciled" (p. 204).

Loewald studied philosophy with Martin Heidegger for three years in Freiberg before he took up medicine. In many respects, Loewald's life's work might be regarded as a kind of Heideggerian reworking of Freud's basic concepts. Nowhere is Heidegger's influence more palpably felt than in the centrality Loewald placed on language. "Language," Heidegger suggested, "is the house of Being. Man dwells in this house" (Steiner, 1978, p. 127). Heidegger regarded modern, technologically based living as shallow and empty. Much of his writings entail the struggle to return to original Greek terms, as a kind of ur-language, in which being once fully resided and that still contains being hidden therein. Loewald similarly regarded contemporary, conventional life as shallow and empty. And Loewald regards the uses to which language is put as embodying and creating different forms of psychic life. The centrality of language in the psychoanalytic experience makes possible a reanimation of psychic life through the excavation and revitalization of words in their original dense, sensory context in the early years of the patient's life.

THE LANGUAGE OF PSYCHOANALYSIS

In what language should psychoanalysis be written and spoken? This has become something of a political issue. Quite a few other theorists less innovative than Loewald have felt that with the shift from drive theory to more interpersonal, relational theorizing, Freud's language, the original language of psychoanalysis, has become anachronistic.[5] Sullivan is an instructive example here. In order to find words to convey his meanings, he decided that traditional psychoanalytic terminology was of no use, because it carried too much baggage. So, he made up many new words. Similarly, Kohut, in slowly introducing self psychology as a radically different analytic model, introduced new terms ("selfobject") and new technical meanings for everyday terms ("mirroring," "empathy"), and intersubjectivity theory has introduced more new terminology ("organizing principles," "developmental strivings") while eschewing traditional words like "drive" and, especially, "projective identification."[6]

Loewald, in contrast, introduced no new terminology of which I am aware. He liked the old words. There are many passages from Loewald that, taken out of context, could easily be mistaken for psychoanalytic writing of the 1930s. Yet the old words he uses all have distinctly, explicitly, different meanings for Loewald. It is precisely his use of old, traditional terminology that has made Loewald's innovations so easy to miss for so many readers. So, why this choice?

There is a passage in a paper Loewald wrote in 1977, the year after the publication of Schafer's (1976) *A New Language for Psychoanalysis,* that hints at the reasons. Schafer's work provides a fascinating counterpoint to Loewald's in this regard. Schafer, who had been supervised by Loewald and whose thinking greatly reflects the impact of Loewald's revision of Freudian theory, had worked under the shadow of Rapaport and the latter's project for organizing Freudian theory and making it systematic. Schafer's (1968) previous book was an extraordinary effort to clean up classical terminology, to make it more precise, to shed its anachronistic features. By the early 1970s, Schafer clearly had given up. He decided that the language of classical psychoanalysis was too saturated with misleading and erroneous meanings, and in *A New Language for Psychoanalysis* he developed a devastating critique of classical metapsychology accompanied by a new language, "action language," which, he argued, was better suited for both theoretical and clinical purposes.

Loewald acknowledges the problems with traditional psychoanalytic theorizing and the usual way in which it is read, but argues against the abandonment of classical terminology. In a clear reference to Schafer, Loewald (1977a) asserts that

> what psychoanalysis needs might not be a "new language" but a less inhibited, less pedantic and narrow understanding and interpretation of its current language leading to elaborations and transformations of the meanings of concepts, theoretical formulations, or definitions that may or may not have been envisaged by Freud [p. 193].

Loewald does not elaborate on the advantages of more imaginative usages of traditional terms, but his understanding of the nature of langauge and its place in development makes it likely that his reasoning went something like this. Freud's language, the language of drive theory, is the archaic language (like ancient Greek for Heideger[7]) of psychoanalysis. It contains within itself, and evokes, powerful affective resonances with both the early infantile, bodily experience it was designed to describe and the revolutionary break-throughs of Freud's genius. At the end of the preface to his collected papers, Loewald (1980) writes, "Freud is close enough to my genera-tion to have been a commanding living force as I grew up and became a psychiatrist, although I never met him in person. He has remained for me, through his writings, that living presence" (p. ix). Freud's living presence, for Loewald, was evoked in the language of his writings (much as his father must have been evoked, I would imag-ine, in the music through which his mother remembered and mourned him).

Rather than finding new words to convey new insights, Loewald nestles his innovations carefully within the old words, giving birth to new meanings while attempting to preserve resonances with a deep past. There is one powerful lyrical passage in "On Motivation and Instinct Theory," an essay dense with metapsychological strug-gles, in which Loewald provides a sense of the enormous power for him of Freud's instinct theory. I quote it at some length because it is so unusual within Loewald's oeuvre and because it provides such a startling glimpse into Loewald's (1980) own passion for Freud's profoundly revolutionary breakthrough.

> *Triebe,* instincts, were—much more than scientists, doctors, ministers, judges ("the educated circles") wanted to admit or know—what made the human world go around, what drove people to act and think and feel the way they do, in excess as well as in self-constriction, inhibition, and fear, in their daily lives in the family and with others, and in their civilized and professional occupations and preoccupations as well. They dominated their love life and influenced their behavior with children and authorities. They made people sick and made them mad. They drove people to perversion and crimes, made them into hypocrites and liars as well as into fanatics for truth and other virtues, or into prissy, bigoted, prejudiced, or anxious creatures. And their sexual needs, preoccupations, and inhibi-tions turned out to be at the root of much of all of this. Rational, civilized, measured, "good" behavior, the noble and kind deeds and thoughts and feelings so highly valued were much of the time postures and gestures, self-denials, rationalizations,

distortions, and hideouts—a thin surface mask covering and embellishing the true life and the real power of the instincts. The life of the body, of bodily needs and habits and functions, kisses and excrements and intercourse, tastes and smells and sights, body noises and sensations, caresses and punishments, tics and gait and movements, facial expression, the penis and the vagina and the tongue and arms and hands and feet and legs and hair, pain and pleasure, physical excitement and lassitude, violence and bliss — all this is the body in the context of human life [p. 125].

The breakthrough quality of this passage, embedded in a very complex, abstract discussion of metapsychological issues, conveys something of the power (language in its "magical-evocative function," pp. 199–200) that Loewald found in a more poetic use of language in psychoanalysis, both in theorizing and in the clinical situation. He noted that poetry (and obscenity) are modes of speaking in which the meanings of the words and the sounds of the words as spoken create an interplay that generates experiences that are *both* cognitive and sensory — embodied understandings.[8]

How should the analyst speak to the patient? Loewald provided virtually no actual clinical examples of his own work, but it is clear that he regarded language in the analytic setting as serving a very different function than that of language used by traditional classical analysts (or by Sullivan, to choose another point of comparison). Traditional classical interpretations were regarded purely in semiotic terms, as a decoding, a translation of the manifest meanings of the patient's associations into latent unconscious meanings. Sullivan, in contrast, regarded the analyst's language in the analytic setting as an investigative tool for getting an increasingly clearer understanding of what actually happened in a particular interpersonal situation. Loewald's concern with regard to langauge is quite different from both of these approaches. He suggests that we use language not only to convey meanings and to clarify situations, but to evoke states of mind, to generate and link domains of experience.[9] A brief clinical vignette of my own might make these differences clearer.

A patient begins analysis because of sleep disturbances with an extremely skeptical view of the whole concept of the unconscious, which he regards as "psychobabble." The first two dreams he reports over the first several months are of frightening underground tunnels into which people disappear and may be lost forever. In his associations to the dreams, he tells me about the backyard of the house in which his family lived during his childhood. There was a septic system under the ground. The tank needed to be drained every so often in a process involving a big truck, at considerable expense and unpleasant smells. The patient's father was an extremely frugal man who defined the family purpose as saving money for the children's educational expenses. Reducing how often the tank needed to be drained would save the family money, and there was a way to make the system more efficient so that the truck was not needed as often. That entailed digging trenches adjacent to the tank and installing "laterals" in the trenches so that there would be more flow out of the tank into the soil. Each summer, the father would lead a family project of digging trenches for more laterals. My patient, starting as a fairly young boy, would be enlisted. His memory of these activities, as virtually all his early childhood memories, was of happy, joyful participation. But there was one memory of his digging at the bottom of one of the trenches, dislodging a rock, and tapping into an underground spring, which began to fill the trench. As he was shorter than the trench was deep, it was with some alarm that he was pulled out while the hole filled with water.

After several months of working on various facets of his current life, filling me in on his history, and discussing his evocative dreams, we hit a lull, and he reported a reluctance to come to his sessions. As I asked him about his reluctance and his feelings about what had been going on, he suggested that he was afraid that I would soon become disappointed in him. "I am just afraid that you will feel I am not working hard enough, not digging deeply enough," he said.

His wording was, of course, quite striking, and I have subsequently come to regard that moment as signaling the emergence of a major feature of the transference. The analytic project in which he and I were engaged had become a symbolic equivalent of his father's "laterals": It was supposed to be good for him, but he had begun to feel the strain of the demands placed upon him. My approval was terribly important to him, and his own self-esteem seemed to have become contingent upon it. The image of the backyard under which all manner of shit was seeping seemed to resonate with recesses in his mind to which he was reluctant to allow himself access. And he was concerned that continued digging might again hit an underground spring and threaten to drown him.

How should the analyst speak about this analysand's "digging"? An interpretation might be called for, pointing to the childhood experiences with the father played out in the transference. The purpose of the interpretation would be to translate the present into the past. Sullivan would have been interested in some digging himself, asking lots of questions about the patient's digging, both in the past and in the present. I imagine Loewald might have been interested in the sound of the word itself and in the physical experience of generating it. I found myself saying the word silently and noting the way in which the sounds of "digging" have an aggressive, penetrating quality that matches the meaning. To say the word, one has to isolate the tip of the tongue against the palate and pull the lips back slightly from one's teeth. The more I thought about it, the more it seemed to me that the meaning, the sound, and the physical activity required to form the word all participated in creating a state of mind and a form of relatedness (first to the father and then to me) that conveyed a constrained, almost harnessed aggressiveness, a homoerotic sensuality (in digging together), and a submission. Rather than stripping the word of the accidents of its original context, it seemed to me that it would be most useful for us to try to resurrect the complex resonances of the word, both past and present, its relational significance, its sexual and aggressive connotations, its capacity to evoke both a state of mind and a subjective world.

REALITIES AND FANTASY

That Loewald was grappling from the beginning with a serious rethinking of fundamental dimensions of the nature of human experience is apparent in a close reading of his earliest papers. In 1949, he read before the Baltimore Psychoanalytic Society a paper entitled "Ego and Reality," in which he teased apart two very different views in Freud's theorizing. In a fashion that was to become the signature feature of his own methodology, Loewald establishes a conventional reading of Freud on the relationship between the ego and reality, and then pieces together an alternative reading that becomes Loewald's own perspective and that is much more interesting.

The conventional understanding of Freud's view of the relationship between ego and reality (or, in a broader sense, between the individual psyche and reality) is that they are fundamentally at odds with each other. The id demands instant relief from the tensions of its drives; external reality, particularly in the social constraints of civilized life, is a dangerous place to seek instant gratification for sexual and aggressive drives. Freud (1923, chapter 2) suggests that the ego grows like a membrane on the surface of the id because the id and its pleasure principle clash irreconcilably with external reality. Thus the ego serves what is primarily a compromising, defensive function, protecting the mind from a reality separate and inhospitable to it; the ego finds largely surreptitious, disguised gratifications for the id's drives as best it can. "This conception of the relationship between ego and reality," Loewald (1980) suggests, "presupposes a fundamental antagonism that has to be bridged or overcome otherwise in order to make life in this reality possible" (p. 3).

Freud's vision of mind and the relationship between instinctual fantasy and perceptions of reality is sharply hierarchical. Fantasy is a lower form of psychic organization, closer to primary process, and subjectivity is saturated with fantasy-based wishes. Accurate perceptions of reality are associated with a higher form of psychic organization, the secondary process; objectivity, of which Freud's beloved science is the apogee, has been decontaminated of fantasy-based wishes. There is in this hierarchical ordering (an analogue of the verbal-preverbal distinction explored in the previous section) an embedded Darwinian metaphor. Ontogeny recapitulates phylogeny; the individual psyche begins with lower life forms (the id) and, mirroring the evolution of species, generates higher life forms (the ego and the superego). Of course, Freud emphasizes repeatedly that human beings cannot simply cut themselves off (through repression) from their primitive motivational underpinnings without the inevitability of neurotic symptoms signaling the "return of the repressed." This is why sublimation, for those blessed with the constitutional talent for it, is such a gift, making possible the gratification of aim-inhibited versions of lower motivations within higher pursuits. The Freudian ego psychology of Loewald's day extended this hierarchicalization of value by adding the concept of drive "neutralization," through which lower sexual and aggressive drives could be cleansed of their instinctual qualities by the ego, which would then use their now decontaminated energies for higher ego functions.[10]

But Loewald suggests there is a second thread, a subtext to Freud's theorizing on these issues, in which ego and reality are not two clashing realms but rather, in the beginning, an original unity. Drawing on one of Freud's passages, to which he returns again and again, Loewald (1949) calls our attention to Freud's (1930) discussion of what he called the "oceanic feeling" at the beginning of *Civilization and Its Discontents*, and argues that

> the relatedness between ego and reality, or objects, does not develop from an originally unrelated coexistence of two separate entities that come into contact with each other, but on the contrary form a unitary whole that differentiates into distinct parts. Mother and baby do not get together and develop a relationship, but the baby is born, becomes detached from the mother, and thus a relatedness between two parts that originally were one becomes possible [p. 11].

Loewald goes on to suggest not only that there is a developmentally early phase of unity between mother and baby (similar to Mahler's notion of a symbiotic phase), but that there is a mode of organizing experience that continues throughout life and in which later distinctions between self and other, internal and external, fantasy and perception are dissolved.[11]

It is crucial to grasp that Loewald did not regard the experience of undifferentiation as illusory or less "real." It is just as real as the differentiating distinctions essential to living adaptively in conventional reality. These are not just developmental phases; they are coterminous modes of experience.

In his last writings, Loewald challenged Winnicott's theorizing precisely on this point. Loewald had been aware that Winnicott's rich notions of transitional space and transitional experience addressed many of the same issues with which Loewald himself was struggling. Goldman (1996) captured well the way in which Winnicott, like

Loewald, attempted to reclaim fantasy as a source of vitality and meaning: "In potential space . . . we come alive as creators or interpreters of our own experience; reality is interpreted in terms of fantasy, and fantasy in terms of reality. Perception renders fantasy relatively safe; fantasy renders perception relatively meaningful" (p. 341).

But Winnicott throughout grants greater epistemological and ontological status to conventional reality. The good-enough mother does not challenge the illusory status the child grants to the transitional object. The good-enough mother meets the child's "spontaneous gesture," making possible the "moment of illusion" in which the child believes she has created the breast herself. Not so, Loewald argues; there is no illusion whatsoever. Winnicott characterizes experiences in these moments as illusions,[12] unreal in reference to an objective, conventional reality in which he himself is anchored. Both children and patients need these illusions to grow with a sense of security (and artists also need these illusions to give free reign to their creativity), but, for Winnicott, they are illusions nonetheless. For Loewald, and this was very important to his whole vision of mind and experience, they are not.

Consider Loewald's (1988) description of the interpersonal event that Winnicott characterized as the "moment of illusion." "Mother and infant may be said to invent each other in the mouth-breast encounter: they come upon something and, out of need or desire, invent-jointly-its utilization" (p. 76). At another point, Loewald challenged Winnicott's claim that the transitional realm, the "intermediate area," takes place *between* inner and outer reality, which Winnicott designated as the province of illusion. "But it is the separation into outer and inner reality," Loewald points out, "that makes for the possibility of 'reality' and 'illusion.' Prior to sorting out inner and outer reality there is no 'room' for an intermediate third area, no space in which to distinguish or oppose illusion and reality" (p. 71).

There are two closely related but distinct concepts that Loewald is illustrating here. First, minds are very closely and complexly interrelated. In the nursing couple, the baby's need for the nursing experience is impossible to separate from the mother's need for the nursing experience. The baby's cry produces a "letting down" response in the mother's breasts; to claim that the baby has, in some sense, created the readied breast is no illusion. The baby's rhythms of hunger and satiety almost immediately following birth are a product partially of the mother's own rhythms of interaction. In the langauge of recent infant research, mother and infant actually *do* cocreate each other through subtle but powerful processes of reciprocal influence.

But Loewald is also making another, even more provocative point. In the baby's experience, and perhaps in some mothers' as well, there is no differentiation between the cry and the response, the mouth and the breast. The nursing experience is one in which self and other are not clearly differentiated. This is difficult to grasp as anything but an illusion, as unreal, because we are so accustomed to thinking of our everyday differentiation of self from other, internal from external, as the sole, incontrovertible reality. Consider, however, some phenomena that are difficult to explain on the basis of this premise.

A woman[13] who recently gave birth found herself holding her baby away from her body, with her arms outstretched, literally at arm's length. She *can* hold the baby in the customary fashion, up against her body with her arms bent at the elbow, but for some reason that she cannot begin to explain, the arm's-length posture seems more natural, more comfortable, more "right." She later finds out that when her own mother was pregnant with her, she was in an automobile accident that broke both her arms. Both arms were in casts, constantly outstretched, for several months after giving birth.

The primatologist Steven Suomi (1995) provides data that seem to bear on this story. Suomi has explored and extended the implications of Bowlby's concept of "attachment" in many different areas. One set of studies considered the question of mothering style in monkeys, attempting to sort out genetic from experiential factors. In precisely the kind of study impossible to do with humans, the researchers separated baby monkeys from their biological mothers and placed them with adopted mothers. They later evaluated the mothering styles of those babies once grown and having babies of their own. The researchers discovered that it was experience, not genes, that was determinative; what emerged was stylistically similar, not to the genetic mother, but to the adoptive mother. Monkeys mother as they themselves were mothered.

In one sense, these kinds of data should not be suprising to psychoanalysts. Since early in the 20th century, Freud used the term "repetition compulsion" to describe the forms through which early traumatic experiences emerge again and again throughout life, often with the roles reversed so that the abused become the abusers. And most of us have had the extremely disconcerting experience of finding the same angry phrases that were hurled at us by our own parents when we were children erupting from our own mouths, as if from a demon that had taken up residence inside of us, in frustrating moments with our own children.

The challenge of these kinds of data is not in the phenomenon of the repetition in adult life of early childhood experiences, good and bad, but in the explanations customarily employed by psychoanalysts to account for them. Something outside of us has been stored inside of us. How did it get there? Analytic theorists have come up with a wide array of terms to account precisely for this phenomena: internalization, internal objects, introjection, incorporation, identification, and so on. These terms are often clinically useful, accompanying explanations for the ways in which external becomes internal, the ways in what was done to people, or in the presence of people, become part of the person himself.

But these explanations seem strained when it comes to accounting for stories like the woman with the outstretched arms and monkey mothering. Do we really believe that the baby whose mother's arms were in casts or the monkey babies clearly perceived the relevant features of their mothers as objects outside of them, and then, through a cognitively sophisticated defensive process, established that image as an internal presence, later identifying with that image of a separate other?

It seems much more persuasive to assume that such early experiences are not stored as images of a clearly delineated external other, but as kinaesthetic memories of experiences in which self and other are undifferentiated. It seems likely to me that what is recorded and stored is a global sense of "mothering," in which the mother and the infant are merged into a singular event that envelops both of them. It may be that many intense emotional experiences, not just in infancy but in later life as well, are organized not only in terms of secondary process, in which internal and external, self and other are clearly delineated, but also in terms of a primary process in which the participants are experienced as cocreating each other. Recent

depictions of the analytic situation in terms of the reciprocal cocrea-
tion of the analysand and analyst in the transference and the countertransference are describing precisely such a process. In Ogden's
depiction of the "analytic third," for example, there is no way to
cleanly separate what the analyst and the analysand are each bringing to the interaction, because each requires the emotional participation of the other (although through different roles) in order to become
actualized in the analytic context.

Consider the difference between an extension of Loewald's approach to these issues and the closely related concept of an "internal
object world" as developed by Melanie Klein. Klein believed that the
infant has elaborate introjective and projective phantasies of movements of substances and body parts back and forth across the boundary between inside and outside. So when I find myself speaking in
irritation to my daughter in precisely the words with which my father
spoke to me, I am identifying with a paternal introject that was
established inside me for purposes of omnipotent control.

In Loewald's vision, by way of contrast, my father's irritated
words were not taken *into* me, they *are* me. I could probably tell you
what was my father and what was me on a multiple-choice test
designed to evaluate secondary process thought. Yet, in those affectively laden moments when they originally happened and when they
reappear decades later, the irritating child and the irritated parent
are, on a primary process level, parts of a singular, undifferentiated
experience. Thus, one could use Loewald's suggestions on these
issues to redefine the phantasies constituting Klein's "internal object
world" as not at all illusory and unreal, but as tapping into a developmental phase and an ongoing mode of experience in which the
customary distinctions between internal and external, self and other,
simply do not apply.

In early childhood, Loewald suggested, fantasy and reality are not
experienced as antithetical to, or even separable from, each other.
Rather, they interpenetrate each other.[14] There is a sense of enchant-
ment in early experience, and an inevitable disenchantment accompanies the child's growing adaptation to the consensual world of
objective reality. Loewald argued repeatedly that it is a fateful error,
which has become a cultural norm, to equate the world of objectivity with the true, sole reality. And psychoanalysis, following the

idolization of science at the end of the 19th century and in the first half of the 20th century, "has unwittingly taken over much of the obsessive neurotic's experience and conception of reality and has taken it for granted as 'the objective reality'" (p. 30).[15] For Loewald, in contrast, an adult reality that has been wholly separated from infantile fantasy is a dessicated, meaningless, passionless world. The traditional Freudian ego psychology of Loewald's day regarded the progressive neutralization of drives and the triumph of the reality principle over the pleasure principle as the acme of mental health. Loewald regarded such a state as a culturally valued, normative pathology. Health for Loewald is a state in which fantasy enchants objectivity, and the past enriches the present.

We have noted that Loewald's radical reworking of the relationship between fantasy and actuality resonates closely with the contributions of Winnicott and others inspired by him. As Marion Milner (1958), drawing on Winnicott, puts it in her book *On Not Being Able to Paint*, "our inner dream and outer perception both spring from a common source or primary phase of experience in which the two are not distinguished, a primary 'madness' which all of us have lived through and to which at times we can return" (p. 28). And along with Loewald, Milner notes that in psychopathology, "we lose the power to endow the external world with our dreams and so lose our sense of its significance" (p. 27).

Consider the everyday clinical question of the relationship between infantile love and adult love. Are oedipal love objects best renounced forever, as suggested by Freud (1924), or does oedipal love perpetually shadow adult passion, threatening to draw adult love into inevitably conflictual incest, as Freud (1930) later suggested? Fromm (1956), following Freud's earlier notion, argued that any vestiges of oedipal, childhood passion in adult love imply neurosis and a failure to engage the present fully. In contrast to Fromm, Loewald, in his most famous lines, detailed the difference between a present that is haunted by the past and a present that is enriched by the past.

The psychoanalytic transference, Loewald (1960) suggests, comes alive as the patient's unconscious tastes "the blood of recognition" (p. 248) in feelings toward the analyst, "so that the old ghosts may reawaken to life" (p. 249). In the neurotic, the past has been improperly buried.

Those who know ghosts tell us that they long to be released from their ghost life and led to rest as ancestors. As ancestors they live forth in the present generation, while as ghosts they are compelled to haunt the present generation with their shadow life. . . . ghosts of the unconscious, imprisoned by defenses but haunting the patient in the dark of his defenses and symptoms, are allowed to taste blood, are let loose. In the daylight of analysis the ghosts of the unconscious are laid and led to rest as ancestors whose power is taken over and transformed into the newer intensity of present life, of the secondary process and contemporary objects [p. 249].

For Freud, transference operated as a resistance to the "memory work" that was the heart of psychoanalysis, the sorting out and decontamination of the past from the present. For Loewald, transference serves as a revitalization, a relinking of the past and the present, fantasy and reality, primary process and secondary process. In Loewald's (1960) vision, the fantasy-saturated primary process of the unconscious and the secondary process of everyday reality need each other. "The unconscious needs present-day external reality (objects) and present-day psychic reality (the preconscious) for its own continuity, lest it be condemned to live the shadow life of ghosts or to destroy life" (p. 250). On the other hand, consciousness and its contemporary objects need links to the affective density of the unconscious, without which "human life becomes sterile and an empty shell" (p. 250). "Our present, current experiences," Loewald suggests, "have intensity and depth to the extent to which they are in communication (interplay) with the unconscious, infantile, experiences representing the indestructible matrix of all subsequent experiences" (p. 251).

In his quiet, undramatic fashion, Loewald (1974a) thereby transformed the basic values guiding the analytic process, substituting meaning for rationality, imagination for objectivity, vitalization for control.[16] The central ameliorative impact lies in relinking.

In the analytic process the infantile fantasies and memories, by being linked up with the present actuality of the analytic situation and the analyst, regain meaning and may be reinserted within the stream of the total mental life. . . . At the same time, as the present actuality of the analytic situation is being linked up with infantile fantasies, this present gains or regains meaning, i.e., that depth of experience which comes about by its live communication with the infantile roots of experience [pp. 362–363].

Consider Kate, a woman in her mid-30s who entered psychoanalysis because of a history of frustrating, abortive relationships with men. She suffered from the not uncommon tendency to choose men who seemed strikingly unavailable for relationships. As we began to sort out some of Kate's experiences, it became apparent that there was something about being in a situation of possible intimacy with a man who might actually be available that made her very anxious; she tended to act extremely self-consciously and find a quick exit. Over the course of the first several months of sessions, as she became aware of these patterns, Kate became a bit more able to bear her anxiety, so that social and romantic experiences of a somewhat better quality became possible.

Interspersed with our focus on her current experiences were accounts of Kate's complicated relationships with members of her family and her early life. She grew up quite poor in a working-class area of a small industrial town. Her father was alcoholic and reclusive, and her overburdened, depressed mother was generally unavailable to her and her several siblings. The mother's mother and brother both lived with the family. At first, the uncle seemed to be an insignificant figure in Kate's development, but little by little I realized how important he was. Unlike the parents, he was somewhat worldly and successful. He owned a car and seemed skilled at enjoying life. He would take other family members out for drives on the weekends, knew about movies and other forms of entertainment, and was a much more exciting figure than Kate's father, who paid very little attention to her. The uncle was a great favorite of the mother, and in many ways filled the vacuum created by the father's withdrawal.

When Kate was several years old, the uncle was arrested for a serious crime. Kate remembered going with her mother to the trial and the enormous grief that enveloped the whole family. The uncle was sent to prison for five years. When he rejoined the family, he was a different man, angry, embittered, burned out. He became tyrannical and frightening. Unopposed by the parents, he bullied the children, and Kate grew to hate him.

I slowly developed the hypothesis that this uncle had been very important to her, not just through fear in her later childhood, but also through positive feelings in her early years. Kate did not like my suggestions along these lines. As far as she was concerned, she hated her uncle and did not even want to talk or think about him.

At about six months into the work, as Kate began to develop a relationship with a man that promised sustained intimacy, she had a series of dreams about the uncle. All she could remember was that they were violent, with yelling and screaming battles like the ones that actually took place during her adolescence. Toward the end of one session, I tried to get her interested in the possible connections between her new, deeper experiences with men and her old experiences with her uncle, reappearing in her dreams. She seemed quite uninterested. I offered an interpretation that went something like this: Her uncle had been passionately important to her in her early childhood; she loved him deeply. His sudden exile was very painful, but her longings for him were kept alive in anticipation of his return. The dramatic changes in him were crushing, extremely painful to her. It became very important never to allow herself to connect with her former loving feelings, because the pain of their loss would have been unbearable. In fact, the fear of the pain connected with her love of her uncle had made all intimacy with all men dangerous. Tolerating loving feelings toward men now, I suggested, would become possible only as she became able to allow herself to reconnect with her abruptly renounced love of her uncle. She allowed that my speculations were interesting, and she left.

At the beginning of the next session, she reported similar dreams about her uncle and said that she had been thinking about my interpretation. Then she fell silent. I asked her what she was thinking about, and she said, with a bit of a twinkle in her eye not uncommon for her, "I am trying to figure out how to convince you that you are all wrong about my feelings about my uncle."

I found myself responding jocularly, "*All* wrong! What do you mean *all* wrong? I figured I wasn't *all* right, but I was pretty sure I got *some* of it right. *All wrong,* boy!" She laughed. I think there was a little more kidding around between us. Then she went on to talk about other things, and we did not return to speaking about the uncle for several months. But Kate's relationships with men continued to deepen.

I have no idea about the impact of that particular interaction; it is so difficult to know. But I find it compelling to think about it in terms of Loewald's way of thinking about the relationship between past and present. Kate's uncle was a ghost, a piece of the past filled with passionate intensity that was split off through repression from her present experience. We might well say that her current relationships with men were haunted by her lost, dangerous feelings toward her uncle. I believe something of that relationship came alive in our interaction. My interpretation was much more complicated and spoken in a more authoritative voice than is my custom. I think there was a kind of teasing in what I took to be the twinkle in her eye and her ambition to prove me "all wrong." I realized afterward that the tone of mock argumentation with which I responded actually derived from my own early relationship with my favorite, very admired, and also very argumentative and opinionated uncle, who could also be playful. I believe Kate and I were working out something about power, negotiation, and play. None of this was self-conscious at the time; the meanings were constructed retrospectively. But I think Kate was experimenting with whether I could wield power differently from the way her uncle did, whether she could back me down. I had become her uncle, but this time we had worked out a different outcome.

In Loewald's terms, a delinking had separated Kate's past from her present, and both suffered. Her past, along with her capacity to play and fantasize in the presence of a man she was excited about, was lost to her. Her present became emptied of depth and vitality. The emergence of ghosts from the past in the transference and in the countertransference made it possible for new links to be opened up.

I conclude this chapter by noting Loewald's definition of reality testing, which dramatically highlights the difference between Loewald's understanding of the relationship between fantasy and reality and the more conventional psychoanalytic understanding. "Reality testing," Loewald (1974a) states, is far more than an intellectual or cognitive function. It may be understood more comprehensively as the experiential testing of fantasy — its potential and suitability for actualization — and the testing of actuality — its potential for encompassing it in, and penetrating it with, one's fantasy life. We deal with the task of a reciprocal transposition [p. 368].

This statement is well worth pondering. Customarily, fantasy and reality are understood as incompatible. Fantasy distorts reality; reality supplants fantasy. Reality testing is conventionally understood to entail an evaluation of ideas for their veridicality: Do they correspond directly to what actually exists? Are they contaminated by the skewing presence of fantasy?

For Loewald, it works quite differently. As with other major dichotomies, like primary versus secondary process, internal versus external, and self versus other, the distinction between fantasy and reality is important to adaptive functioning. But separating fantasy and reality is only one way to construct and organize experience. For life to be meaningful, vital, and robust, fantasy and reality cannot be too divorced from each other. Fantasy cut adrift from reality becomes irrelevant and threatening. Reality cut adrift from fantasy becomes vapid and empty. Meaning in human experience is generated in the mutual, dialectically enriching tension between fantasy and reality; each requires the other to come alive. In the psychic universe of the individual mind, vitality and meaning require open channels between the developmentally earlier, but perpetually regenerated primal density and the clearly demarcated boundaries that make possible adaptive living. For Loewald, only the enchanted life is a life worth living.

CHAPTER 2

DRIVES AND OBJECTS

In a series of dense, tightly reasoned metapsychological essays over the course of three decades, from the 1950s through 1970s, Hans Loewald worked on and worked out certain central, difficult problems that were of great concern to him: the nature of mind, the relationship between actual events and psychical internality, and the revitalization and transformation of the past within current experience. It would not be too reductive to say that Loewald was working on problems of being and time, and putting it that way highlights the impact on Loewald's work of the three years he spent studying philosophy with Heidegger in Freiberg. But if the problems that gripped Loewald were Heideggerian, the conceptual world that he lived in and loved was Freudian.

Loewald had a profound respect and deep passion for the psychological explorations Freud undertook and the conceptual tools Freud gave us for investigating, thinking about, and talking about unconscious processes. Yet Loewald clearly felt that Freud's theories were not tidy, final explanations, that he had opened up a largely uncharted realm that was left to us to explore. And there were fundamental problems in Freudian theory, problems of being and time, that Loewald was gripped by and felt required attention. Loewald believed that Freud's own grasp of these issues was lacking, inevitably so, because of Freud's place in time and the history of ideas. It was always important to Freud to reaffirm the scientific status of psychoanalysis and the objectivity of his discoveries, and to systematize whatever his flashes of intuition had illuminated by making his metapsychological systems consistent with the biology and physics of his time. So Freud's metapsychology lumbered along, like a wagon train behind a scout, colonizing, according to the fashions of the day, newly opened territory.

But it was precisely in the assimilation of Freud's insights into the intellectual conventions of his day, and our day as well, that Loewald felt some of the most remarkable implications of Freud's discoveries remained undeveloped. Loewald reminds us repeatedly that in a genius as fecund as Freud's, there are always multiple meanings, contradictory positions, subtexts, unexplored paths. And the problems in which Loewald was interested often required a return to just those points in Freud's work where imaginative clinical leaps had been harnessed into familiar intellectual conventions. Loewald returns, again and again, to pick up the thread, to venture down the road not taken.

Loewald felt that the dominant interpretations of Freud's work by the Freudian authorities of his (Loewald's) day were woefully inadequate. Loewald was working during the heyday of structural theory and ego psychology, and although it was not his nature to become involved in ideological disputes, it is clear that Loewald had serious problems with both of these approaches. In a review of *Psychoanalytic Concepts and the Structural Theory* by Arlow and Brenner, a book that was to become a pillar of the then contemporary Freudian structural theory, Loewald (1966) concluded: "Many unsolved and obscure questions of psychoanalytic theory look as though they were now taken care of and cleared up. This approach simplifies theory at too high a price, for the gain of a smooth, neat surface" (p. 58). And although Loewald sometimes identifies himself with "ego psychology" as the dominant ideology of his day, his ego psychology is clearly different from the mainstream ego psychology grounded in Hartmann's work. In fact, as we noted in the previous chapter, Hartmann often operates as the unspoken antagonist in many of Loewald's essays.[1] And Loewald's final book, *Sublimation,* was in many respects an alternative approach to Hartmann's concept of "drive neutralization" as a bridge between primary drives and human intellectual and cultural achievements. Thus, Loewald's contributions are located within and saturated with Freud's thinking, but it is not the Freud of the Freudian authorities of Loewald's day. It is not even Freud as Freud understood himself.

Reading Loewald is tricky. The language is Freud's, but the meanings have often been changed, slowly, from one paper to the next. And a consideration of Loewald's theory of object relations, the subject of this chapter, requires us to plunge into a thicket of the most contested, rhetorically burdened terms of all: instincts, drives, objects, and object relations. Therefore, we need to stick close to Loewald's own language and careful arguments. I hope to show that in his struggle with basic problems of Freudian theory, Loewald presented us with a vision of mind and relationships with others that in many respects anticipated much of current psychoanalytic thinking and in some respects provides us with a visionary glimpse of human experience the implications of which we are still struggling to understand. Like Freud, Loewald can be read differently, from various angles; like Freud, he can be read in pedantic or imaginative ways. What I am most interested in, ultimately, is not the philosopher's Loewald but the clinician's Loewald, the illumination that Loewald's contributions provide contemporary analytic clinicians in our current struggles with the complexities of the analytic process.

DRIVES

There are two features of Loewald's commitment to Freud that are particularly striking. First, Loewald believed that the central feature of Freud's contribution was his theory of drive—his uncovering of the instinctual, primitive, "lower" sources of human motivation. Second, Loewald believed that there was something fundamentally wrong with the way drive was understood, both by Freud and by mainstream psychoanalysis.

In a review of the Freud–Jung correspondence, Loewald (1974b) makes clear this dual concern in his appreciation of Jung's contributions on spirituality and self-transformation, which overlap, in many significant respects, Loewald's own interests, particularly his final work on sublimation. Yet, Jung's abandonment of Freud's unmasking of the seamier, primitive roots of human experience was a serious blunder.

Psychoanalysis, I believe, shares with modern existentialism the tenet that superpersonal and transcendental aspects of human existence and of unconscious and instinctual life [so much stressed by Jung] can be experienced and integrated convincingly—without escapist embellishments, otherworldly consolations and going off into the clouds — only in the concreteness of one's own personal life, including the ugliness, trivialities, and sham that go with it [p. 416].

Despite the interest he shared in "higher" transformations of the human spirit, it was essential to Loewald never to forget the "lower" sources of motivation that Freud's revolution had uncovered, his unmasking of our intricate hypocrisies, and his revelation of the body-based underbelly of all our activities, the body in its full corporeality, in its surfaces, its parts, its excretions. Loewald reads Jung as enjoining us, like the Bishop of Yeats's *Crazy Jane* poems, to "Love in a heavenly mansion, / Not in some foul sty." But Loewald responds to Jung like Crazy Jane responded to the Bishop:

> 'Fair and foul are near of kin,
> And fair needs foul,' I cried.
> . . . .
> . . . Love has pitched his mansion in
> The place of excrement;
> For nothing can be sole or whole
> That has not been rent [p. 255].

Yet, despite the extraordinary power of Freud's vision, his blend of fair and foul, there was, for Loewald, something fundamentally off about the way Freud typically thought about drives. This had to do with beginnings, the locus and origination of experience.

Freud said many, many different things about drives and instincts and early experience. But throughout, Freud felt that an appreciation of man's biological nature, our Darwinian bedrock, entailed granting the origination of experience to body-based instinctual impulses. The "source" of drives, as he put it, is in a body part. Drives emerge from the body and make a demand on the mind for work. The locus of activity begins *within* the individual and pushes outward toward the world. The id predates the ego, which grows like a membrane on its surface, to shelter the id from externality and to mediate its interface with the outside world. The center of the individual, despite our thorough socialization over the course of development, is in the id. "The core of our being, then, is formed by the obscure *id*, which has no direct communication with the external world and is accessible even to our own knowledge only through the medium of another agency" (Freud, 1940, p. 197). Life for Freud is generated through the clash between the id and the external world, and it is precisely because of that fundamental incompatibility that the id itself never directly meets the external, interpersonal world. As Jay Greenberg (1996) has put it, "Freud is expressing a vision in which human development and its psychopathology are rooted in the collision between organism (drive, thing) and environment (object, word). Personality is formed in this collision and is therefore always a tragic compromise" (p. 891). It is precisely the nature of the drives as presocial and asocial that links Freud to one line of his intellectual ancestors — the romantics — and operates, as Rapaport (1958, p. 727) pointed out, as a hedge against the pull toward adaptation and socialization.

Despite its explanatory power and appeal, there was, for Loewald, something fundamentally wrong with this vision. Perhaps *the* central feature of Loewald's revisions of Freudian theory is his shifting the locus of experience, the point of origination, from the individual to the field within which the individual comes into consciousness, and this has been making its way into contemporary Freudian thought. In the beginning, Loewald says over and over, is not the impulse; in the beginning is the field in which all individuals are embedded. Experience does not proceed, as Freud believed, from inside outward, from the id's impulse, through the ego, into negotiation with the outside world. Experience initially moves from outside inward, from an increasingly differentiated unity of which the individual is a part to the development of the individual through an internalization of those external patterns.

Loewald found the authority for this basic reconceptualization of the nature of drives in Freud's reference to the "oceanic feeling" in the opening of *Civilization and Its Discontents* (1930). Romain Rolland had challenged Freud's critique of religion as infantile by evoking the mystical experience of oneness. Freud responded by suggesting that life begins in an experience of boundarylessness: "Originally the ego includes everything," Freud states, "later it separates off an external world from itself" (p. 68). Perhaps this early condition is reexperienced in mystical states, Freud conceded, although he himself reported never having had such moments. Freud's depiction of the origins of the ego in this passage, so important to Loewald, is difficult to reconcile with what might be regarded as the major trend in Freud's portrayal of the ego in other works, in which the ego is an early developmental achievement. If the ego arises on the surface of the id to mediate between the id and the external world, it is hard to imagine how the ego in the beginning could also include the external world. This is one of those points at which the richness of Freud's imagination exceeded his efforts at theoretical integration.

But the passage from *Civilization and Its Discontents* became the centerpiece of Loewald's revision of the concept of drive. If experience begins in a boundaryless unity, Loewald reasoned, mind, at its fundamental levels, cannot be composed of body-based impulses emerging from the individual and clashing with the external world. The very experience of being an individual mind and an individual body distinct from other minds and bodies — all this is a secondary development, a reorganization. And that changes the very meaning of the term "drive," leading Loewald (1972) down a road very different from those Freud traversed.

> Instincts or instinctual drives . . . arise within and develop from a psychic matrix or field constituted essentially by the mother-child unit . . . not as biological forces, [but] as forces that *ab initio* manifest themselves within and between what gradually differentiates into individual and environment (or ego and objects, or self and object world . . .). Instincts remain relational phenomena, rather than being considered energies within a closed system, to be "discharged" somewhere [pp. 152–153].

In Loewald's view, Freud began to shift from his earlier energic-discharge (Loewald sometimes refers to it facetiously as Freud's "fuel-injection") notion of drive to a relational notion of drive in 1920 with the introduction of the concept of Eros in "Beyond the Pleasure Principle." This shift, however, was never complete, and Freud's relational model of drives remained a secondary, largely undeveloped avenue. But it was central to Loewald's project and recently has been further developed in the contributions on Eros in the writings of Jonathan Lear (1990, 1998).

Consider some of the redefinitions of basic drive theory terms that derive from Loewald's reconceptualization of drives as relational rather than energy-discharge phenomena.

The terms "primary" and "secondary" process have "a deeper meaning," Loewald (1972) suggests, than in their original usage as modes of energic regulation.

> Mental and memorial processes are primary if and insofar as they are *unitary*, single-minded . . . undifferentiated and nondifferentiating, unhampered . . . by laws of contradiction, causality, and by the differentiation of past, present, and future and of subject and object, i.e. by the differentiation of temporal and spatial relations [pp. 167–168].

Thus, the term "primary process," Loewald suggests, should be used in reference to the original state of the infant-mother field, in which there is no organization as such, in which all the usual distinctions that make possible our ordinary experience are missing. "The secondary process is secondary insofar as in it *duality* becomes established, insofar as it differentiates; among these differentiations is the distinction between the perceiver and the perceived" (p. 168).

In secondary process, Loewald suggests, the relational field has become organized, and temporal and spatial distinctions have become established. Secondary process does not emerge spontaneously by itself; it is introduced to the child by caregivers. It should be noted that secondary process cannot ever exist independently of primary process; it presumes an underlying unity that it organizes and differentiates. "The secondary process," Loewald (1977a) suggests, "consists not simply in splitting, dividing, discriminating, . . . but that in this same act the original wholeness is kept alive by an articulating integration that makes a textured totality out of a global one" (p. 196).

In Freud's drive model, the term "cathexis" refers to an investment of energy. In Loewald's (1977a) relational drive model, cathexis refers to organizing activity. Different kinds of cathexes refer to different ways in which the relational field can be organized. Thus,

> object-cathexis is not the investment of an object with some energy charge, but an organizing mental act (instinctual in

origin) that structures available material as an object, i.e. as an entity differentiated and relatively distant from the organizing agent. Such a cathexis creates — and in subsequent, secondary cathecting activities re-creates and reorganizes — the object *qua* object. It is *objectifying* cathexis [p. 195].

It is crucial to note here, and we soon take this up in greater depth, that Loewald is taking pains to suggest that objects, in a psychological sense, do not exist independently of the subject. Objects are created by being invested with significance through organizational (object-cathectic) activity out of the "primal density" or primary process.

Similarly, Loewald suggests,

narcissistic cathexis . . . is not investment of a pre-existing ego or self with some energy charge, but a mental act (instinctual in origin) in which "available material" is not differentiated from the cathecting agent, not distanced in the cathecting act; the cathexis is *identificatory*, not objectifying [p. 195].

In object cathexis, one is drawing a boundary around a piece of experience, differentiating something out, and saying, "This is you." In narcissistic or identificatory cathexis, one is drawing a boundary around a piece of experience, differentiating something out, and saying, "This is me."

It should be apparent that through all these redefinitions the very sense of "drives" has been radically transformed. The id, the repository of drives, is no longer understood as the initiator of motivation and, as Freud put it repeatedly, cut off from the external world; for Loewald, the id and the drives are relational patterns through which experience is organized. In one of my favorite passages from his classic paper on "On the Therapeutic Action of Psychoanalysis," Loewald (1960) suggests that far from being a hedge against social forces pulling for adaptation, the id is itself created through mutually adaptive interactive processes. Like the remains of a buried city, the fragments may be unrelated to current social reality. But those fragments were hardly pushed up from the center of the earth. Like primary process, they are residues of a once richly interactive social life.

To use Freud's archeological simile, it is as though the functional relationship between the deeper strata of an excavation and *their* external environment were denied because these deeper strata are not in a functional relationship with the present day environment; as though it were maintained that the architectural structures of deeper, earlier strata are due to purely "internal" processes. . . . The id—in the archeological analogy being comparable to a deeper, earlier stratum—integrates with its correlative "early" external environment as much as the ego integrates with the ego's more "recent" external reality. The id deals with and is a creature of "adaptation" just as much as the ego—but on a very different level of organization [p. 232].

OBJECT AND OBJECT-RELATING

What is an object? For Freud, objects are other persons, or body parts, or things that have been discovered to be useful in reducing the tension of drives. For Klein, objects are a kind of teleological image wired into drives themselves, like Jungian a priori archetypes toward which desire is inherently directed, which then become psychically intermingled with real others and parts of others in the external world. For Fairbairn, reversing Klein, objects begin as real others in the external world toward which "object-seeking" libido is directed, which may defensively and compensatorily become transformed into internal presences. In all these accounts, objects exist as either real external entities or prewired properties of experience.

Loewald's understanding of "objects" is quite different from *all* these accounts. For Loewald, experience begins in an undifferentiated state; there are no objects, no drives, no self, no others, no now, no then, no external, no internal. Everything is experienced in terms of what Loewald calls a "primal density." All the distinctions and boundaries with which we are familiar are superimposed upon this primal density.

One of the central psychoanalytic questions has always been "Why do we seek objects?" (see Greenberg, 1991). There have been many different answers: pleasure, safety, attachment, recognition, and so on. In Loewald's perspective, the question actually does not make sense. It presumes "we" and "objects" are separate phenomena. Yet, "In the formation of the ego," Loewald (1949) suggests, "the libido does not turn to objects that, so to speak, lie ready for it, waiting to be turned to. In the developmental process, reality, at first without boundaries against an ego, later in magical communication with it, becomes objective at last" (p. 19). For Loewald (1971a), we *are* our objects, and our objects are us. The distinction between drives and objects is a developmentally later, secondary process superimposition upon the primal density in which self and other are not yet sorted out.

> Objects are not givens. On the contrary, a highly complex course of psychic development is required for environmental and body-surface stimuli to become organized and experienced as external, in contrast to internal, and for such sources of stimulation, gratification, and frustration eventually to become objects [p. 127].

Loewald later concludes:

> Objects are "originally connected" with instincts in such a way that the problem is not how they become connected in the course of time and development, or why they become connected. Rather, seen from the standpoint of instinctual life, the problem is: how what later is distinguished as object from subject, becomes differentiated, in the course of mental development, from instincts [p. 136].

This crucial point may seem abstract and difficult to grasp, but it is actually quite familiar to any interpersonally oriented psychoanalyst or couple or family therapist. Consider the way things work in couples or families. We are all fundamentally conflicted about all the major issues of life: seeking versus regulating pleasure; expressing versus restraining aggression; spending versus conserving money; rededicating versus reopening commitments, and so on. We all contain intense feelings on both sides of all these issues. But as couple and family relationships are often structured, one or the other side of these fundamental universal conflicts is assigned to different persons. One partner wants a commitment and the other evades it; one family member spends recklessly while another patrols expenditures; one child expresses the family outrage while the other is a model of virtue; one partner seems to want sex all the time while the other seems to avoid it. What goes on here? Each participant individually (and collaboratively with other participants) creates his own subjectivity and creates his objects by superimposing on the rich, affective, conflictual density of experience a simplifying scheme, through sorting out and assigning different qualities to different participants. It is just this sort of layering process, Loewald is suggesting, through which secondary process is generated out of primary process.

Consider the implications of this novel theory of the origins of objects and object relations for Loewald's understanding of the crucial processes of internalization, projection, and identification. In virtually all other psychoanalytic theory, internalizations, projections, and identifications are discrete acts, generally understood as ego defenses. The paradigm for this understanding was Freud's (1917) formula that identification follows abandoned object cathexes — identification and internalization are defenses against the pain of loss.[2]

What is distinctive about Loewald's approach is that objects are not sought, or found, or taken inside, or expelled. In the beginning, there is no outside or inside. We are one with our objects; objects and self emerge out of the material of dense, affectively laden experience. Let us see if we can clarify some of the implications of this difference in theory through a thought experiment.

Picture yourself waking up in a room adjacent to various other rooms with other people and things. You go into one of those and bring that person back into your room, thereby "internalizing" him, or bring some things that were in other rooms back into yours, thereby "internalizing" those properties that you now can claim as yours. This is the traditional model of objects and internalization.

Now picture yourself in a large space with several other people and many things all jumbled together. No distinctions exist; everything is yours; there *is* only yours. Let's call this state of affairs "primary process." Later, you start creating boundaries and borders around some of the other people and things. Some you put in rooms of their own, separate from you. Others you keep in your space. Others are in in-between spaces with two-foot-high room dividers. Let's call this more complexly differentiated state "secondary process." Finally, let us assume that these room dividers are made of some sort of translucent material, so they are both there and not there; they can be felt in some sense modalities but also disappear in others. This is Loewald's model.

For Loewald, internal objects and identifications *begin* as you; their sense of otherness is a product of secondary process differentiations and sorting. But primary process is operative not just in the earliest months of life; it is an ongoing organization of experience. At one point, surely evoking Heidegger, Loewald (1978a) suggests that the primary unity of experience might "best be called being" (p. 36). Primary process, in its undifferentiated unity, operates as a level of organization, simultaneous and parallel to the secondary process that dominates our consciousness with its differentiated objects. "It is this interplay between unconscious and consciousness," Loewald suggests, "between past and present, between the intense density of undifferentiated, inarticulate experience and the lucidity of conscious articulate experience, that gives meaning to our life" (pp. 49–50).

In the traditional model, internal objects and identifications were created when you moved objects and things from other rooms into yours, and projections were created when you moved things from your room into others. In Loewald's model, there was no moving around, only different patterns of organization. Self and other are created by selectively drawing boundaries around some features of experience and excluding others. The experience of self is generated in the identificatory process of creating internality; the experience of otherness is generated in the projective process of creating externality. Of course, this analogy can take us only so far. The imaginary rooms are about the relationship between mine and not-mine. Psychoanalytic models of the psyche are about the relationship between me and not-me.

Thus, for Loewald, the distinctions between self and other, internal and external, are psychological constructions. The *inter*personal and the *inter*subjective are secondary constructions, developmental achievements, generated out of an underlying, undifferentiated psychic field, in which there are no persons and no subjects. And *internal* objects are also secondary constructions. The "other in oneself" as Loewald (1978a) puts it, is, "only the end product of a complex differentiating—from another viewpoint, self-alienating—process that takes its start in the primary unity of the infant-mother psychic matrix" (p. 14).

Mind for Loewald (1965) is like a viscous psychic medium, within which relational configurations, interactions with others, are suspended and continually assimilated into the self and alienated from the self. "Internalization . . . is conceived as the basic way of functioning of the psyche, not as one of its functions" (p. 71). Internalization (like sublimation in Loewald's later writings) is sharply contrasted with defensive processes. "In internalization, in contrast [to repression,] the ego opens itself up, loosens its current organization to allow for its own further growth" (p. 75).

On higher levels of organization, objects have a vivid sense of otherness, of externality. On more primary levels of organization, the divisions are thin and permeable. Over time, externality may dissolve altogether as object libido becomes narcissistic libido and others become self. Significant interactions with early caretakers transcend the dividers between internal-external, now and then. Thus, for Loewald, the distinctions between internal and external, self and other are not objective features of the way the world is, but constructions on a gradient of possible constructions. Objects, or rather our interactive experiences with objects, take on varying degrees of internalization and externalization. Consider Loewald's (1972) description of early identifications, in which he is arguing against the traditional notion that internalizations are distinctive defensive responses to loss and deprivation.

Early identifications with the parents occur under circumstances that have nothing to do with deprivation or loss, but with a closeness amounting to lack of separateness, as though what is perceived or felt in this intimacy, by that very lack of distance, becomes an element in the child or helps to form his character—as though the parent's trait is continued into the child, without his having to give up anything [pp. 162–163].

Loewald envisions mind as a latticework of interactive identifications, simultaneously in different degrees of assimilation on different levels, with a sense of self on one side and a sense of externality on the other. This vision has close connections to contemporary relational notions of multiplicity of self-states and self-organizations (Mitchell, 1991; Davies, 1996, 1998b; Bromberg, 1998).

Loewald's theory of object formation solves what for me was always one of the most interesting unsolved problems in psychoanalytic theorizing. *Why* are the residues of early object relations so persistent and resistant to change? It is just this feature of human psychology that makes our work so difficult, that necessitates such long stretches of time. Freud could describe it, but he couldn't really explain it. His metapsychological pleasure principle claims that we seek pleasure and avoid pain. Yet, the durability of early traumatic experiences and relationships is probably the most widespread psychological cause of human suffering. Polymorphously perverse libido, in all its plasticity, should be able to discard painful objects and find new ones. Yet the depth of our loyalty to painful early objects (which was the clinical basis for Fairbairn's redefinition of libido as not primarily pleasure-seeking but as object-seeking), which we encounter over and over in analysis and life in general, is staggering. Freud attributed this phenomenon to what he termed the "adhesiveness" of the libido, but threw up his hands at a compelling explanation by attributing it to a mysterious Death Instinct. And Meltzer (1975) used this same word, which I have always found so experientially vivid, in describing "adhesive identifications" in autistic states. What is so marvelous about Loewald's theory is that it dramatically reframes the whole problem. Primary identifications are so adhesive because there is a boundary between me and my objects only on a conscious, secondary process level of organization; on a primary process level, I *am* my objects, and my objects and I are always, necessarily, inseparable. They can never be expelled. This suggests that what can happen in psychoanalysis, what does happen, is not renunciation or exorcism of bad objects, but a transformation of them.

TIME AND MEMORY

Self and objects are related to each other in Loewald's model of mind through interactions, and interactions are related to each other through time. To approach Loewald's understanding of time, which, like most other things, soon departs from conventional understandings, let us consider what he has to say about the complex, reciprocally generative relationship between perception and memory.

What is the difference between perception and memory? Memories, Loewald (1978a) suggests, are experiences that have an "index of pastness" (p. 66), and perceptions are experiences that convey a quality of the present. But memories were once perceptions; they reproduce perceptions, which reverberate through them like echoes. And perceptions would not be possible without memories. Adult cataract patients whose vision is restored have no way to organize what they are looking at; the completely novel is indecipherable. We can only perceive something by re-cognizing it in terms of past perceptions, or memories.[3]

Thus, internal object relations, the internalized interactions with others that are the latticework of mind, are bound together in time. Time is the basic fabric of the psyche. And memory, Loewald (1972) suggests, is that psychic activity that traverses those temporal fibers, making links, continually creating channels through which "interactions with the world continue to reverberate" (p. 156) in a way that makes self-reflective, personal experience possible. Memory, Loewald suggests, is

> the central, all-pervasive activity of the mind by which our world and our life gain breadth and depth and continuity in flux, and change in continuity, by which, in other words, our life and world acquire dimension and meaning, [making] memory virtually synonymous with mind itself [p. 149].

Once again, these distinctions, which sound very abstract, are extremely rich clinically. Consider the way in which we work with memories in the analytic situation. The patient may associate to an earlier time, his fifth birthday, let us say. That is clearly past, not present, a memory, not a perception. But in what Loewald (1978a) calls "poignant remembering" (p. 66), with which we are most frequently involved in clinical psychoanalysis, we might ask the patient to see if he can get in touch with what that birthday was like, what it felt like. Our hope is that the earlier state of mind is not just being represented in an intellectual fashion, but to some extent being reexperienced.

> As we become absorbed in such memories not only do we lose, as we say, the sense of time and space, but we tend to repeat, relive, internally and in our imagination, what we perhaps wanted only to recall as past events. . . . In all such experiences, while our rational processes may continue to operate and to articulate the material of experience, at the same time another level of our mind has been touched and activated [pp. 66–67].

We have seen that Loewald believed that self-other and internal-external are secondary constructions upon a parallel organization in which self-other, inside-outside are undifferentiated. Similarly, he also believed that our experience of time as duration — past as distinct from present as distinct from future — is a secondary construction upon a parallel organization in which these temporal categories do not exist. It is only as boundaries between self and other are constructed that past and present are also distinguished: "in a deeper sense, only by virtue of the differentiation of subject from object — which is the primordial separation — does memory arise" (Loewald, 1972, p. 160). Yet, just as with the boundary between self and other, the boundary between present and past exists only on a secondary, not a primary process level. Thus, the present and the past, perception and memory always retain their Siamese relationship (see also Grotstein, 1981) with each other, joined on one level and differentiated on another. Perception and memory, Loewald suggests, are bound together, necessarily, in a dialectic of reciprocal influence.

In our customary way of thinking about these things, past, present, and future are discrete categories reflecting the objective passage of time as a succession of moments, one after the other. For Loewald, feelings of past, present and future are constructions that create a sense of before, now and after, and provide answers to the questions,

What happened? What is happening? What will happen? Each of the concepts — past, present, and future — has no meaning in itself. Past in relation to what? Present in contrast to what? They imply each other, and create a subjective sense of connection, a narrative scaffolding for organizing experiences. According to Loewald (1971a), "We encounter time in psychic life primarily as a linking activity in which what we call past, present and future are woven into a nexus . . . the nexus itself is not so much one of succession but of interaction" (p. 143). What we experience as our mind itself is the result of the continual regeneration of the links[4] between past and present. Loewald (1972) states that "interactions with the world continue to reverberate, are reproduced, and thus lay the foundations for the development of an internal world, in the form of memorial processes" (p. 156). And, as a true constructivist, Loewald suggests that mind is continually, actively reconstructed through linking. "That this linking activity is automatic and unconscious in most of our daily life," Loewald (1971b) suggests, "obscures the fact that it *is* an activity" (p. 145).

THE ANALYTIC PROCESS

Because Loewald writes about analytic process only in the most abstract terms, and his writing lacks virtually any clinical examples, it is impossible for analytic clinicians who have fallen under the spell of Loewald's extraordinarily rich vision to discern how Loewald himself actually worked. But I am not even sure this matters. As McLaughlin (1996) notes,

> What has made Loewald's writings so beckoning to many of us is that he provided theoretical grounds to support a far broader range of technical activities than those sanctioned in the 1960s by the classical viewpoint in whose language he spoke. In his implicit clinical depiction of the working analyst, he shaped idealizing and appealing images about what a good analyst would wish to be. Yet these images are quite encompassing, making it easy for each of us to read into his depictions our own particularities, shaped according to our individual aspirations, and affirming of our preferences [pp. 901–902].

For our purposes here, I want to briefly address the implications of Loewald's revisions for the two most basic features of the analytic process: the analytic situation and the analytic relationship.

Loewald views the human psyche in radically interactive terms. Our minds are open systems embedded in an interactive matrix with other minds, and our sense of self is a function of the internalization and continual reproduction and memorialization of those relationships. Loewald (1960) stresses repeatedly "the role that interaction with environment plays in the formation, development, and continued integrity of the psychic apparatus" (p. 221). In traditional terms, as Loewald describes them, the analytic situation is a medium within which the "closed system" of the patient's mind is revealed and interpreted by the analyst operating "as a reflecting mirror . . . characterized by scrupulous neutrality" from a vantage point outside that system (p. 223). In Loewald's vision, the analytic situation is an open, interactive matrix, in which the analyst is "a co-actor on the analytic stage" (p. 223). And interaction is the key, previously unexplored feature that Loewald stresses over and over, with the implication that "a better understanding of the therapeutic action of psychoanalysis may lead to changes in technique" (p. 222).

But how open is open when it comes to the analysand's engagement with the analyst as a real person in the analytic situation? And how open is the analyst as a psychic system encountering the patient? There are places where Loewald seems to suggest a radical, mutual openness and engagement indeed, suggestive of the kind of unique intersubjective mix Ogden writes about in connection with his term "the analytic third." The analyst, Loewald (1977a) suggests,

> is, on the now pertinent level of the patient's mental functioning, drawn into this undifferentiated force field . . . he has to be in touch with that mental level in himself, a level on which for him too, the distance and separateness between himself and the patient are reduced or suspended. Ego boundaries, the whole complex individuating organization of self-object differentiation tend to dissolve [p. 379].

To return to our earlier analogy, we might say that the analyst joins the patient in the undivided room of primary process, or that the patient and analyst slowly come to find and differentiate themselves and each other collaboratively in an undivided room.

Loewald (1974a) makes it clear that it is the lived reality of the transference-countertransference experience and its interpretive understanding for both participants that makes deep change possible. The analyst's role is not one of "detached spectatorship"; Loewald stresses the importance of "the analyst's capacity and skill of conveying to the patient how he, the analyst, uses his own emotional experience and resources for understanding the patient and for advancing the patient's access to his, the patient's inner resources" (p. 356). Thus memories become revived as perceptions, ghosts are raised, and new and different perceptions generate different, less dissociated memories, as ghosts are transformed into ancestors. "It is thus not only true that the present is influenced by the past, but also that the past — as a living force within the patient — is influenced by the present" (p. 360).

Consistent with his understanding of the analytic process as interactive, Loewald recommends that the analyst engage the patient in lively terms, without the traditional restraints that come with aspiring to an impossible objectivity and neutrality. He frequently compares the analyst's role to that of the parent, not so much the mother of the infant as in the British school of object relations, but most often the parent of an adolescent. "So-called educational measures, and at times encouragement and reassurance, are used. If used judiciously they often make possible and enhance the more strictly psychoanalytic interventions in all phases of an analysis" (Loewald, 1977b, p. 375).

Although Loewald warned against the dangers of infantilizing the patient through overuse of developmental metaphors,[5] he has come under fire by contemporary relational critics for infantilizing the patient and also (to borrow a pun from Phillip Bromberg, 1998) "for adult-erating" the analyst (p. 144). In consistently portraying the analyst as, necessarily, a "mature" object, Loewald grants a privileged status to the analyst that rings false to many contemporary ears. The deconstruction, in recent decades, of the automatic assumption of the analyst's maturity, along with all other forms of authority, makes Loewald's attribution unpersuasive. Even a cursory glimpse inside the politics of analytic institutes and associations quickly reveals that psychoanalysts are not paragons of maturity.[6]

Loewald was writing at a time when analysts of all persuasions took for granted that the analyst's analysis made him or her more rational and mature, developmentally more advanced than patients. In this respect, I think that this criticism of Loewald and his contemporaries is well founded. But I think Loewald's critics are missing something and this concerns, as it usually does with Loewald, the particular meanings he attributes to words we tend to assume have commonly understood meanings.

Yes, Loewald regards the analyst as more mature than the patient, but what does he mean, exactly, by "maturity"? Maturity for Loewald is not the customary advanced position along a linear developmental scale; for him, maturity is the capacity to navigate among and bridge different developmental and organizational levels. Consider this passage from Loewald's (1949) earliest psychoanalytic paper, which presages so much that was to follow.

> It is not merely a question of survival of former stages of ego-reality integration, but that people shift considerably, from day to day, at different periods in their lives, in different moods and situations, from one such level to other levels. In fact, it would seem that the more alive people are (though not necessarily more stable), the broader their range of ego-reality levels is. Perhaps the so-called fully developed, mature ego is not one that has become fixated at the presumably highest or latest stage of development, having left the others behind it, but is an ego that integrates its reality in such a way that the earlier and deeper levels of ego-reality integration remain alive as dynamic sources of higher organization [p. 20].

Loewald (1977b) thus portrays the analyst not as solidly, consistently parental, but as straddling levels of organization.[7] "The difference between the patient and the analyst is that the former is at the mercy of that primitive level (inundated by it or disavowing it), whereas the analyst is aware of but not given over to it" (p. 379). In the recent psychoanalytic literature, different authors strike different sorts of balances in depicting the contrast between the analyst's surrender to primary process and the analyst's maintenance of at least some foothold in secondary process. Loewald often seems to assume considerable control on the analyst's part over his own participation, although in his final work (1986) he seemed to be stressing increasingly the dangers of rationality as screening out unconscious communication and the sense that the analyst's control is, necessarily, episodically lost and regained.

I find it compelling to make use of Loewald's contributions on the analytic situation by distinguishing analysand and analyst, not in terms of characterological levels of maturity, but in terms of the difference in their roles and the impact of those differences on the states of mind that become available to them. As Lear (1998) points out, for Loewald, "the psychoanalytic field is constituted by a differential in psychological organization: the analyst is more highly organized than the analysand" (p. 133). But, consider Loewald's (1974a) very careful choice of words in the following passage; what he is conveying here is complex.

[The patient] knows that he has come to another adult for help, hoping or trusting that the analyst is more experienced, more knowledgeable, and more mature in regard to emotional life than he himself. As an adult the patient also knows that he is not altogether the child he makes himself out to be, or the child he lets take over in the regressive pull of the analytic situation [p. 362].

The patient "hopes" the analyst is more experienced, knowledgeable, and mature in regard to emotional life. In contrast, the patient "makes himself out to be" a child in the "regressive pull" of the analytic situation. Loewald is tracing the ways in which the different roles shape the greatly overlapping experiences of patient and analyst in different ways. The analyst, in his assumption of professional responsibility, also hopes he is more mature and knowledgeable and tries to act that way, much as a parent might with a child with whom he is emotionally enmeshed. The patient does not have to be responsible and organized in this way; in fact, we consider the patient who is trying to be responsible in this way to be resisting the precious opportunity the analytic situation provides for a freedom from conventional accountability, a surrender (Ghent, 1992) to unintegration. Loewald regards as essential for the analytic process the analyst's capacity to bridge primary and secondary process, self and other, past and present, reality and fantasy.

Thus, the relative maturity that Loewald assigns to the analyst vis-à-vis the patient is not so much concerned with the content of experience—not primarily a difference in the organizational level on which the two operate—but rather with a relatively greater facility for navigating shifts and convergences between different levels of experience. The patient, for extended stretches between interpretations, is encouraged to suspend that facility; it is a central feature of the analyst's professional responsibility to keep bridging concerns always in mind. These differences, and the dialectic between expressiveness and restraint they generate in the analytic process, are taken up in the final chapter.

For Loewald, the analyst's own internal bridges among his own differentiated but linked levels of organization make possible the creation of an interpersonal analytic situation that becomes patterned, within the transference-countertransference, into revitalized islands of disparate dissociated experiences of the patient's. And these interpersonal patterns in turn become internalized for the patient (to some extent for the analyst as well) into a newly enriched, internal world. Consider one of my favorite of Loewald's (1977b) depictions of the analytic process. My hope is that this chapter may have contributed to making what might have seemed quite abstract, now richer in its primordial referents.

> Psychoanalytic interpretations establish or make explicit bridges between two minds, and within the patient bridges between different areas and layers of the mind that lack or have lost connections with each other, that are not encompassed within an overall contextual organization of the personality. Interpretations establish or re-establish links between islands of unconscious mentation and between the unconscious and consciousness. They are translations that do not simply make the unconscious conscious or cause ego to be where id was; they link these different forms and contents of mental life, going back and forth between them. . . . What is therapeutic, I believe, is the mutual linking itself by which each of the linked elements gains or regains meaning or becomes richer in

meaning — meaning being our word for the resultant of that reciprocal activity [p. 382].

Loewald (1978a) revealed himself somewhat more in his Yale lectures for the general public than in his professional writings. There he said, and I would like to end this chapter on this note, that "one does not have to be a mystic to remain open to the mysteries of human life and human individuality" (p. 25).

PART II

LEVELS OF ORGANIZATION

CHAPTER 3

AN INTERACTIONAL HIERARCHY

The basic features of Loewald's vision of mind are held in common, generally explicitly, sometimes implicitly, by other relational theories: human minds are interactive phenomena; an individual human mind is an oxymoron; subjectivity always develops in the context of intersubjectivity; we continually process and organize the enormous complexity of ourselves and our world into recurring patterns.

To say that an "individual mind" is oxymoronic is to say that no individual human mind can arise sui generis and sustain itself totally independent of other minds. This does not belie the fact that individual minds do arise out of and through the internalization of interpersonal fields, and that having emerged in that fashion, individual minds develop what systems theorists call emergent properties and motives of their own. Thus, in an earlier paper (1988) I distinguished between field-regulatory and self-regulatory processes. In the beginning, we might say, is the relational, social, linguistic matrix in which we discover ourselves, or, as Heidegger put it, into which we are "thrown." Within that matrix are formed, precipitated out, individual psyches with subjectively experienced interior spaces. Those subjective spaces begin as microcosms of the relational field, in which macrocosmic interpersonal relationships are internalized and transformed into a distinctly personal experience; and those personal experiences are, in turn, regulated and transformed, generating newly emergent properties, which in turn create new interpersonal forms that alter macrocosmic patterns of interaction. Interpersonal relational processes generate intrapsychic relational processes which reshape interpersonal processes reshaping intrapsychic processes, on and on in an endless Möbius strip in which internal and external are perpetually regenerating and transforming themselves and each other.

There is, as we have seen, an additional, extremely important and provocative concept that can be culled from Loewald's contributions, one that has had less common currency: our minds organize our experiences according to different principles, varying organizational structures. These organizational schemes emerge sequentially over the course of development, but they also operate simultaneously in adult experience on a continuum from consciousness to unconsciousness. Loewald most often contrasted primary process and secondary process "levels of organization," varying according to degrees of articulation of spatial boundaries between self and other, inside and outside, and temporal boundaries among past, present, and future. Ogden (1989) has more recently introduced a similar vision of mind, organized, simultaneously, in different "modes": autistic-contiguous, paranoid-schizoid, and historical. Ogden's modes, like Loewald's levels, vary according to degrees of articulation of spatial boundaries around the self and between self and others, split versus whole object relations, reality testing, and awareness of the irreversibility of time. Like Loewald, Ogden understands these modes as emerging sequentially in early development, but also as operating in dialectical tension with each other throughout the life cycle. One mode is in the conscious foreground of experience at any one time, but the others are also always processing experience in their own terms.

The project of this chapter is to draw on these principles to introduce four different modes or categories for housing and comparing different perspectives on, and accounts of, relationality.[1] I will propose four interactional dimensions, four basic modes through which relationality operates. Like Loewald's distinction between primary and secondary process, and like Ogden's modes of autistic-contiguous, paranoid-schizoid, and historical, the modes I am teasing apart and delineating increase, progressively, in degrees of organizational sopistication. Mode 1 concerns what people actually *do* with each other — nonreflective, presymbolic behavior, the ways in which relational fields are organized around reciprocal influence and mutual regulation. Mode 2 is shared experience of intense affect across permeable boundaries. Mode 3 is experience organized into self-other configurations. Mode 4 is intersubjectivity, the mutual recognition of self-reflective, agentic persons.

Different relational authors tend to place their emphasis, to locate their conceptual center of gravity, in one or another of these dimensions. Thus, for example, Bowlby was most interested in behavior: what mothers and children actually *do* with each other. He was also certainly concerned with affect, self-other configurations, and intersubjectivity, but these were derived from what he regarded as the fundamental, instinctual behavioral patterns of attachment. Fairbairn was most interested in self-other configurations: libidinal and antilibidinal egos in relation to objects. He also had a great deal to say about behaviors, affects, and intersubjectivity, but these were understood as derivatives of underlying internal object relations. Benjamin (1988, 1995, 1998) is most interested in intersubjectivity: the development of a sense of self as a personal, agentic subject in relation to other personal, agentic subjects. She is also concerned with behaviors, affects, and self-other configurations, but contextualizes these other dimensions on a trajectory through which intersubjectivity emerges.

The relational framework suggested in this chapter is offered as a heuristic device for locating, juxtaposing, and integrating different kinds of explorations of different dimensions of relationality. It is not meant to be a Procrustean conceptual scheme, and does not claim to carve nature at its joints. One can sort out different interactive notions and theories in many different ways. I am hoping to demonstrate that the project of juxtaposing different relational dimensions in a hierarchy of increasingly sophisticated organizational patterns is useful, for a critical synthesis of relational concepts, for thinking through the clinical implications of interaction within the analytic situation, and for exploring some of the choices clinicians make daily about what to say or not to say about what they are feeling and what they are doing.

MODE 1: NONREFLECTIVE BEHAVIOR

People in recurrent relationships coconstruct behavioral patterns of interaction involving reciprocal influence. In developing his interpersonal theory, Sullivan was particularly interested in this phenomenon: what people actually *do* with each other, who is doing what to whom. Clinically, this sort of analysis has been extensively explored by more interpersonally oriented writers (e.g., Levenson, 1972, 1983), employing the sort of method Sullivan referred to as a "detailed inquiry" to track the subtle choreography of interpersonal microadaptations, generally within the "here-and-now" dimensions of the analytic relationship. This behavioral dimension was also central in Bowlby's (1969) attachment theory, in which the powerful bonds that develop between small children and mothers are understood to derive from instinctive activities, such as sucking, clinging, and smiling. Bowlby regarded these behaviors as "mediating" attachment by evoking complementary maternal behaviors on the part of the caretaker, which in turn evoke other bonding behaviors. In this relational methodology, intimate relationships are constructed in a complex choreography of behaviors in which participants cyclically cue and respond to each other in turn. Although focused on behavior, authors exploring this sort of approach are by no means "behaviorists"; they have been as interested as any psychoanalysts in what goes on inside people's minds and internal worlds. But they tend to regard a close tracking of what people are actually doing with each other as a promising route in.

This mode of interaction has been dramatically demonstrated by contemporary infant researchers who have traced the complex gestural, behavioral cueing between mother and infant that comes to regulate the infant's sleep-wakefulness and feeding cycles. Patterns of reciprocal influence are generally either preconscious (out of awareness, but subject to being known) or unconscious (out of awareness and warded off, hence inaccessible). This organization has generally been characterized as presymbolic (Beebe et al., 1997) or prereflective (Sander, in press), in that actions and interactions function without an organized conceptualization of self and other. On this level, the question, Who started it? is meaningless, because the actions of each participant have evolved, through microadaptations, in complementarity to those of the other.

Daniel Stern and his colleagues (1998) have recently adapted the kind of empirical approach developed in infancy research to small sequences of analytic interactions, tracking what they call "relational moves," leading up to transformative, coconstructed "now moments." (For an exploration of psychoanalytic applications of infant research, see Kumin, 1996.)

This emphasis on what has been called "procedural knowledge" or, more recently, "implicit relational knowing" is invaluable clinically. Analytic work often gets bogged down in speculative interpretations of what things mean; clinical interventions that illuminate what is actually going on in the patient's life and, in particular, in the interaction between the patient and analyst are often extremely powerful. The richness of recent dynamic systems approaches derives from its exploration of the dialectics between complexity and unity, differences and continuity, change and recurrence. In any dynamic system of the sort constituting a parent-child or analyst-analysand dyad there is a continual recurrence of patterning and also continual change. Analytic interpretations often reflect a reductionism that collapses the complex textures of experience to highlight the compulsion in the repetition compulsion. Systems approaches like Sander's encourage us to see the recurrent patterning and, at the same time, appreciate the novelty, the creativity in repetition. It provides a rich vision of process that undercuts any reductive tendencies to collapse affectively dense interaction into singular causes. As Ghent (in press) has recently noted in an illuminating discussion of dynamic systems theory, "The power of dynamic systems theory lies in its transcendence, by virtue of its insistent focus on process, of such age-old controversies as nature vs. nurture, mind vs. body, causes vs. reasons, etc."[2]

MODE 2: AFFECTIVE PERMEABILITY

Affect is contagious, and, on the deepest level, affective states are often transpersonal. Intense affects like anxiety, sexual excitement, rage, depression, and euphoria tend to generate corresponding affects in others. Early in life, and on the deepest unconscious levels throughout life, affects are evoked interpersonally through dense resonances between people, without regard for who, specifically, is feeling what. Questions like, Who started it? and Who did what to whom? are often useful to ask at other levels of organization. But these questions tend to be meaningless when intense affective connections are involved, as in strong sexual attraction, terror, murderous rage, or joyous exhilaration.

This fundamental, boundaryless, affective level of experience has been noted and explored by different analytic authors from different traditions. Harry Stack Sullivan, back in the 1930s, wrote about what he termed "the empathic linkage" through which feeling states are transferred, in a kind of contagion, from caretakers to small children. Sullivan's intuitions in this area have recently been dramatically demonstrated in empirical studies of affect transmission between mothers and infants (Tronick et al., 1978; Demos, 1999). As we have noted in chapters 1 and 2, Loewald, in his metapsychological revision of primary process experience, suggests that powerful emotional experiences are registered in a fashion in which what *I* am feeling and what *you* are feeling are not sorted out independently, but rather form a unity, the totality of which I experience as me, which can be reexperienced in moments Loewald (1978a) terms "poignant remembering" (p. 66).

Mode 2 experiences, in which direct affect resonances emerge in interpersonal dyads, have been explored in the recent psychoanalytic literature, in the interpenetrability of transference-countertransference experiences, in which the analyst's own affects are understood as a window into the deepest, often dissociated affective experiences of the patient (Ogden, Bollas, Bromberg, Hoffman, Mitchell, Davies).

MODE 3: SELF-OTHER CONFIGURATIONS

Interpersonal experiences are organized into configurations entailing self in relation to others. Sullivan called them "me-you patterns"; ego psychologists speak of "self and other representations"; Kernberg's terms are "self-other-affect configurations." On this symbolic level of organization, coconstructed interactions are sorted out and tagged, consciously or unconsciously, according to the persons involved. Thus, I am in one sense my mother's son, and in another sense my father's son. In each of these relationships, I have both shaped myself in relation to my parents and internalized a sense of my parents in relation to me. There are times when I feel (consciously or unconsciously) like my father's son relating to my father, and other times when I feel (consciously or unconsciously) like my father (through identification) relating to me, his son. There are times when I feel (consciously or unconsciously) like my mother's son relating to my mother, and other times when I feel (consciously or unconsciously) like my mother (through identification) relating to me, her son. Furthermore, I am in one sense the son of my mother's conscious, and in another sense the son(s) of my mother's unconscious conflicts. Similarly with my father.

Fairbairn's theory of internal object relations played a central, generative role in opening up this approach to interaction; he introduced two invaluable principles that have been extensively developed in the recent literature. First, self-formation and other-object formation are inseparable. Because libido is "object-seeking," it makes no sense psychologically to think of a self except in relation to an other. And because others become psychically relevant only when invested by the self, it makes no sense to think of objects outside of relationships with versions of the self. The second principle inherent in Fairbairn's vision, which has been made explicit and elaborated in contemporary theorizing with respect to the self (Ogden, Mitchell, Bromberg, Davies, Aron), is that we are multiplicitous, not a single self struggling with warded-off impulses, but discontinuous, multiple self-organizations packaged together by an illusory sense of continuity and coherence that has both conscious and unconscious features. In contemporary relational theory, these multiplicitous organizations are much more than (cognitive) representations of self; rather, they are each versions, complete functional units with a belief system, affective organization, agentic intentionality, and developmental history.

It should be noted that all three of the modes we have considered so far might be considered in terms of Kohut's concept of selfobjects. In each of these three modes, others are not organized and experienced as independent subjects in their own right. In Mode 1, others participate in recurrent, often stabilizing patterns of interaction that are neither symbolized nor reflected upon; in Mode 2, others participate in affective connections, sometimes making certain kinds of affective experiences possible; in Mode 3, distinct others are symbolized, but play specific functional roles, like mirroring, exciting, satisfying, and so on. Only in Mode 4 are others organized as distinct subjects.

MODE 4: INTERSUBJECTIVITY

Being fully human (in Western culture) entails being recognized *as a subject* by another human subject. There is a deep, ongoing tension between our efforts to have our own way, as an expression of our own subjectivity, and our dependence on the other, as a subject in her own right, to grant us the recognition we require. In Mode 3, experience is sorted out iconically in terms of persons; in Mode 4, the persons, both oneself and others, have become more complex agents, with self-reflective intentionality (thinking about and trying to do things) and dependency (upon other agents for completion).[3]

It has become commonplace to note that, traditionally, theorizing about the anlytic process placed the analytic *relationship* in either a minor, subsidiary role, or left it out entirely. The analytic situation was not understood as an engagement of two persons, but as a medium within which the mental content of one person unfolded and was interpreted by another person operating as a more or less generic, objective functionary. In the broad sea change in the ways in which the analytic process is now understood and envisioned, the analytic relationship, the personal relationship between the two participants, is now granted a fundamental, transformative role. Several major theoretical traditions and contributions have played a role in this pervasive paradigm shift.

From (British middle-group) object relations and self psychology theorists has come a replacement of the more paternal and patriarchal classical psychoanalytic metaphors for the analyst's role by postclassical metaphors for the analyst's role as an (often romanticized) maternal presence: holding, containing, empathizing. A problem with these contributions has been that the analyst still remains a generic functionary, albeit of a more appealing sort. We might say that analytic action here is still understood within a Mode 3 framework.

From interpersonal psychoanalysis has come an iconography of psychoanalysis as a much more personal, truly intersubjective, "authentic" encounter. Once one gets past the word "interpersonal", however, there have been problems imagining how such an encounter actually works. The two dominant influences on the development of interpersonal psychoanalysis as a clinical tradition were Harry

Stack Sullivan and Erich Fromm, whose sensibilities were conveyed much more through an oral tradition and generations of supervisees than through their writings. And Sullivan and Fromm had very different clinical sensibilities. Sullivan himself seems to have had two different styles (see White, 1977), depending on whether he felt he was encountering a patient suffering from schizophrenic or from neurotic difficulties in living. With schizophrenics, Sullivan was extremely careful, one might almost say delicate. He regarded schizophrenics as poised always on the edge of utter humiliation and was deeply respectful of their brittle shreds of self-esteem. This current of Sullivan's work dovetailed with the remarkably empathic and devoted approach that Frieda Fromm-Reichmann (1950) developed in her work with schizophrenic patients at Chestnut Lodge. With neurotics, however, and with supervisees (see Farber, 1999), Sullivan was often extremely sarcastic, sometimes brutal. He seems to have regarded neurotic "security operations" as a form of nonsense from which patients were usefully disabused. Along somewhat similar lines, Fromm (1994) placed great importance on frankness and honesty. He felt that people in our culture systematically deceive themselves and each other about how they really feel. Fromm envisioned the patient as coming to analysis to hear the truth, and he regarded the analyst's role as primarily the deliverer of that truth.

The tradition that has recently come to be known as Relational Psychoanalysis (Mitchell and Aron, 1999) reflects a blending of these diverse currents into a broad, multidimensional vision of human intersubjectivity. From the interpersonal tradition there came a humanity and a precious emphasis on personal involvement and authenticity that remained undertheorized and lacked both a developmental rationale and a rigorous framework of considerations for its constructive application. From the object relations traditions there came a textured developmental perspective and rationale for a constructive restraint, but the lack of a place for the more active forms of the analyst's personal engagement.

And a major contribution to Mode 4 theorizing on intersubjective dimensions of relationality has come from relationally oriented psychoanalytic feminists like Jessica Benjamin and Nancy Chodorow. Prior psychoanalytic developmental theorizing has tended to portray the goal of development as separation and autonomy, and the mother (and, by analogy, the analyst) as an object of the child's needs (e.g., the "need-gratifying" mother of classical drive theory or Winnicott's "holding environment"). But, Benjamin and Chodorow demonstrated, a more meaningful vision of health both for the child (and for the psychoanalytic patient) is a sense of subjectivity and agency, in the context of relatedness and recognition by, and identification with, a mother (analyst) who is a subject in her own right.

FEELINGS IN THE AIR

The patient's relationships with others, including the analyst, have become a major focus of psychoanalytic inquiry. Important relationships are enormously dense and complex, with many different facets, useful to explore in many different ways. The four-tiered, interactive hierarchy we have been considering is helpful in sorting out some of the different kinds of relational phenomena usefully brought under analytic scrutiny.

Charles has been in analysis for several years. His relationships with women had become depressingly redundant. He found not being in a relationship intolerable, and would become obsessed with the hunt for a girlfriend. He was adept at evoking women's interest in him and would become easily infatuated, particularly with someone somewhat remote or inaccessible. As the current woman became more interested in him, he entered a thicket of dense ruminations about whether she was, in fact, the right woman for him, about whether he was really excited by her and did indeed love her. The more he ruminated, the less he felt for the woman and the more suffocated he became by the woman's feelings for him. Toward the end of the cycle, he longed for the escape that ending the relationship would provide, so that he could be free to hunt a variety of women once again. But almost as soon as he found himself unattached, he would begin to court a new commitment.

Over the course of several years of analysis, the futility of this pattern became increasingly clear to him; he was able to remain for periods of time in situations where he could suspend his metalevel obsessions about whether he felt enough for the woman he was with to actually have more authentic feelings for her. For almost a year, he had been with Sarah, with whom he had experienced stretches of pleasurable experiences of some intimacy. She then confronted him with a dilemma. They were at the point in their relationship where, she felt, they should be saying to each other, "I love you." She had said it several times, and he seemed to have withdrawn. So she stopped saying it. Sarah, who struck me as a woman of considerable emotional maturity, was not interested in coercing protestations of love from Charles. But she felt that the fact that such verbal expressions of love were not forthcoming was not unimportant and probably put a ceiling on what was possible in their relationship.

Sarah's confrontation created something of a crisis for Charles, and he, and then he and I, spent quite a bit of time trying to sort out exactly what he *did* feel about her in different situations. There were times, he noticed, when "love is in the air." I became very intrigued about what this meant, and sorting it out became helpful to me in distinguishing the different modes of organization I have introduced in this chapter, because these were experiences in which all four modes were operative simultaneously.

These moments when love was in the air often followed intense shared experiences, like engrossing conversations or exciting sex. It was an affective outcome of complex, interactive sequences between them in which they were both active participants, both presymbolically (Modes 1 and 2, in the subtle choreography of successful emotional and sexual intimacies) and symbolically (Mode 3, in the conscious and unconscious ways in which they had come to understand each other and themselves in relation to each other). The love that was "in the air" was a feeling that was clearly an interactive product of the relatedness between them; but who, exactly, was feeling what?

The most familiar, easiest way for Charles to approach this question was to assume that Sarah, not he, felt the love; he felt *her* feeling love for him and therefore felt pressured to declare a love he did not really feel. But, we came to understand, that description did not really do justice to the situation. It was not easy for him to know what he felt, because he felt so obliged to gratify and control what he imagined was her need for him (he fantasized about taking a polygraph test to discern what, in fact, he did feel). When he could free himself from his largely self-imposed pressure to say things he did not feel, he came to realize that he certainly did feel something for Sarah in these moments. But was it love? It had elements in it, as he struggled to sort them out, of warmth, dependency, gratitude, security, and exhilaration. But was it love? *Does* the feeling of love come in a prepackaged form, waiting to be correctly identified and named? Or does the naming itself make it into love? (See Spezzano, 1993, for a consideration of this and many other dimensions of the dynamics of affect.)

One could approach this situation via the concept of projective identification. Of course Charles loves Sarah, we might assume, but he is too anxious to allow himself that feeling. So he projects his love into her, experiences it coming from her, and controls it *in* her by distancing himself from her. Love is "in the air" because that is where Charles projects it. There is some value in this formulation, but it is also misleading. The love that Charles felt *in* Sarah was not just his projection; it was not just a fantasy of his affect residing in her. She also seemed, in fact, to be feeling love for him at those moments. The more we explored the situation, the less useful was the effort to choose between the view that the love "in the air" was *her's*, which he was afraid of, or *his*, which he evacuated outside the boundaries of his experience of himself. We were speaking, so it seemed, about affective experience that could exist only if it operated in both of them, an experience that required two participants to ignite and fuel. So, in an important sense, this feeling they have in relation to each other *is* "in the air"; it is not simply in either or both of them; it has a transpersonal quality and operates in the field that they comprise together, Mode 2, in shared affect across permeable boundaries.

Yet, there is an important difference in the ways in which Charles and Sarah are processing or organizing their affect. Sarah wanted to say, "I love you," and she also wanted Charles to say this to her. The more Charles and I mulled over the implications of Sarah's wish, the clearer it became that saying "I love you" is not just a report on a prepackaged feeling, but also a linguistic "performative" (Havens, 1997). Saying "I love you" has, built into it, various other messages and actions. It says, "I like loving you"; "I want to love you"; "I accept and embrace my loving you"; "I want to evoke an expression of what you might be feeling for me." Saying "I love you," that is, operates in Mode 4 as a fully developed intersubjective event. It is self-reflectively self-defining and calls for a recognizing response of one sort or another from the other. In this sense, Sarah was right. Saying "I love you" or something equivalent to each other is not just a report on what has happened; it contributes to determining whether their relationship will deepen or whether certain paths of development will be foreclosed.

THE EMBEDDEDNESS OF AFFECT AND PROCESS

Among the most difficult features of the human experience is coming to terms with both our relational embeddedness with others (in the interpersonal field) and the embeddedness of others within our own minds (in the internal world). Because of the pervasive relationality of our emotional lives, we have much less control over our own affective experience than is generally comfortable for us. Our emotions and our behaviors have, to some degree, a messy life of their own, in the gaps, the spaces, between oneself and others. Charles's obsessive ruminations about what he was feeling were partly in the service of trying to wrestle illusory control over the open interpersonal space that love requires in order to thrive. The "omnipotence of thought" that Freud (1913) identified in this sort of obsessive maneuver runs like a red thread through virtually all forms of psychopathology, representing a wide array of efforts to control psychic experiences that, because of their fundamental relationality, simply cannot be controlled.

For most of its history, psychoanalytic technique was based on the premise that the patient's psyche and mental processes could be "analyzed" independently of their interactions with the analyst's feelings and behaviors. The latter, it was presumed, could be factored out or held constant through proper technique. In the framework I am proposing, traditional concepts (e.g., projective identification) are recontextualized as components of a more complex interactive field. Because they are like stop-frame, spotlighting manipulations of a fluid process, they become misleadingly reductive when applied as exclusive accounts. Thus, in my view, projective identification is bidirectional, not a unidirectional process, with affective, fantasy, and behavioral features (see Seligman, 1999). Affects are not substances residing inside minds, but rather transpersonal, interactive processes that are organized variably with behaviors, self and other experiential units, and, on higher levels of organization, folded into a subjective sense of agency.

The interactional hierarchy I have been sketching out highlights the complex, textured two-person nature of emotional experience, in which there is a great deal happening at once: feelings, actions of varying complexities, shifting experiential configurations, and self-reflective agency. The distinctions among the modes is offered as a heuristic device for sorting out the strands.

Contemporary clinical psychoanalysis has become a blend of traditional and innovative features. Free association, the patient's dreams, and the analyst's interpretations — these all still have a central place. But because the analyst is understood as influencing and cocreating the process, no matter what she attempts to do, there also tends to be more open, less restrained moments of interaction with the patient. In traditional analytic technique, rigor was maintained by efforts to avoid interaction (Gill, 1994); in contemporary relational technique, rigor is maintained by continual reflection upon interaction that is assumed to be inevitable and by conducting oneself in those interactions in a fashion aimed at maximizing the richness of the analytic process. Analytic change is understood not simply as an intrapsychic event: insight generated by the analyst's interpretations. Analytic change is now understood as beginning in changes in the interpersonal field between patient and analyst, as new relational patterns become interactively cocreated and subsequently internalized, generating new experiences, both with others and in solitude.

AFFECT: CONTROLLED AND UNCONTROLLED

Becky, a 30-year-old woman in the fifth year of intense and productive analytic work, reminded me of something I had said six months earlier, which, she declared, had become an "epiphany" and had an enormous impact on her. I had offered a rather traditional interpretation of her fantasied omnipotence; the retrospective importance she granted to that interpretation led me to reflect upon the factors that might have contributed to its particular significance for her.

Becky had begun analysis in a state of considerable confusion and drift, both in her personal relationships and in her career. She had

had a difficult childhood in many respects. Her mother was a college professor who was quite depressed and considered herself a failed scholar; she regarded any successes on Becky's part as a profound threat. Her father, a corporate executive, was a lively, flirtatious man who had had open affairs with considerably younger women during Becky's adolescence. Through her adolescence, there had been an intense, seductive tension between the two of them, about which she felt intensely ambivalent and guilty. "Your body is just the same as your mother's when I fell in love with her," was the sort of thing he would say to her during her adolescence, in the context of discussing the death of his sexual relationship with Becky's mother. Becky experienced both parents as extremely self-absorbed and concerned only about appearances, oblivious of her inner life.

Over the course of our work together, Becky had returned to school and was pursuing an advanced degree in history. About nine months earlier, three months prior to the interpretation in question, she had expressed considerable anger at me. I had been missing how much trouble she was having, she claimed. Perhaps I was misled by her apparent success at school, not noticing how depressed and anxious she often felt about how blocked she was in the papers she was supposed to be writing. Perhaps, like her parents, I was more interested in appearances and my own values than in her inner experience and happiness.

I thought there was some truth to Becky's charge as well as a revival of important features of her relationships with her parents. We explored some of the ways in which she and I had recently been drifting along into a jointly created sense of complacence regarding her external successes. We had created (Mode 1) reciprocal behavioral patterns in which things looked good on the outside, but painful experiences were overlooked. As a result of this discussion, we focused more intensely on her current struggles, which included her blocked writing projects. She was reluctant to describe these in any detail, because they entailed technical material and controversies that she regarded as both arcane and tedious. She could not imagine I would be interested. But I was, partly because I am genuinely interested in the methodology of history and partly because I thought it might be an important route to understanding her current difficulties.

There ensued several months of on and off discussions of the topics of her papers. Occasionally I knew something of what she was struggling with, but most of the time I encouraged her to explain to me the issues and controversies—in effect, to teach me. She was hesitant at first, but as we went along, she was able to speak more freely; I was increasingly impressed by her brilliance and creativity, which I had never been able to glimpse first-hand. In Mode 4, there was an expression of her own originality and my recognition of it. I found these sessions very lively, informative, and fun, sometimes almost exhilarating. In Mode 2, there was a shared excitement at the play of ideas between us. Of course, with the guilt that is part of any psychoanalyst's repertoire, I worried that I was exploiting Becky for my own edification, and, of course, to some extent I was. But these discussions seemed important, and as we proceeded she came more to life and her writing problems eased. It seemed important to me *not* to interpret what was going on between us at that point. Nevertheless, I felt we had managed to cocreate a kind of experience she had never had with her parents, whose narcissistic concerns and investments made an enjoyment of Becky's own creativity either irrelevant or too threatening. (In Mode 3, there emerged an expansive and powerful version of herself reflected in an appreciative and contributing other.) After a while, the focus of our inquiry moved onto other topics.

In the session of the impactful interpretation, Becky was reflecting on her progress over the past several months. She was feeling better in many ways and no longer stalled in her work. Yet, she still felt both pessimistic about ever feeling really likable and also felt especially cynical about men. She knew how to get people to like her, she remarked, especially men. Because she had learned social graces from her parents, she could be quite charming, and because she was quite beautiful, she could dependably arouse men's sexual interest in her. But how would she ever feel that anyone really liked her for herself?

We had been over this ground several times before, including an exploration of her ambivalence about whether or not to believe that I found her sexually attractive. On one hand, she wanted to believe that she had captivated me through her charms, because that made her feel special and valuable in a way with which she was familiar, but she simultaneously did not want to believe she had captivated me through her charms, because that would cheapen our relationship in a way with which she was familiar. What I said at that point was something like this: "I think people, including men, sometimes like you very much for reasons over which you have absolutely no control." She reacted thoughtfully at the time to this interpretive statement, but did not bring it up again for six months, during which time her depression lifted further and her relationships with men became increasingly less tortured. Now, looking back, she noted how powerful my remark had been for her.

What had happened? My statement might be regarded as an interpretation of Becky's conflictual ambivalence. Spelled out with all its implications, it conveyed something like this: You imagine you have omnipotent control over the impressions others have of you. This is partly an accurate appreciation of effective interpersonal strategies you developed as a child and partly a fantasy you developed to ward off anxiety. But others have feelings about you outside your control, and if you could give up your need to believe in your own omnipotence, you might find that interesting and satisfying.

But why did this remark, not so different from other interpretations made at many different points, matter so much at this precise juncture of the treatment? We will never know, but I imagine it was partly the result of what had been taking place between us in the previous months: Becky had felt the sense of heightened affective engagement (Mode 2) between the two of us in the discussions about her papers. She and I together had found a way to interact (Modes 1 and 3) that granted much greater focus to her inner experience, both pain and creativity, than she had access to before. Earlier, like both her parents, I had been somewhat absorbed in my own concerns and values (Mode 1), distracted from noticing the depth of her struggle with her writing. Later, unlike her mother, I felt sufficiently unthreatened to enjoy her talents and accomplishments; unlike her father, I could share an excitement and pleasure with her without leaving her feeling manipulated and controlled. Nevertheless, before the interpretation, Becky had drawn these new experiences into old (Mode 3) "me-you patterns" of her omnipotent control over the excitement she aroused in others. In making the interpretation, it was clear to both of us that I was not delivering an abstract piece of understanding, but expressing my own feelings about her, which opened up the possibility of a new "me-you pattern" and also provided a degree of (Mode 4) intersubjective recognition that had not previously been experienced.

In an early dream there had been a group of mothers holding damaged babies who all looked like generic, vapid "Barbie" dolls. The mothers were expressing outrage about the harm that had come to their babies and were trying to bury them; but the babies kept rising up out of their common grave, only to be brutally clubbed by the mothers over and over again. Becky and I both found this image a powerful representation of the interpersonal world of her childhood, as well as of the continual self-brutalization she inflicted upon herself in her inner world. Her parents' concerns with appearance and envy of her vitality and creativity were smothering to any sense of self and personal worth, and, through internalization, she had become bound up with her mother in a perpetual cycle of self-attack and desperate efforts at regeneration. In our affectively laden interactions over her writing, Becky and I had managed to open up this closed, repetitive circle generating new experience, both interpersonally and internally.

The meaning of the interpretation of omnipotent control for Becky rested upon the shared experiences of the prior three months of discussions about her writing projects. There were clearly elements of reenactment in those sessions with respect to both parents. Something was being experientially reexplored vis-à-vis the mother regarding how freely Becky's own intellectual potency might operate without evoking my demoralization and retaliation. And something was being experientially reexplored vis-à-vis the father regarding how freely and pleasurably we might intellectually play with each other without her feeling either exploited to enhance my own self-esteem or dropped when I tired of her. There were elements of quasi-seduction present as well, although it would have been difficult to determine whether she was seducing me or I was seducing her into seducing me.[4]

What if I had not inquired into her blocked writing projects? Would this have been a more neutral stance? Hardly. It would likely have been experienced as a reenactment of her parents' self-absorption. Within current relational theory, there is no way for the analyst not to act and, in one way or another, to reenact as well. What is crucial (Gill, 1994) is a continual self-reflection on the dense, multiple reverberations of the past in the present and a commitment to forms of interaction that seem most enhancing to the patient's developing vitality and sense of freedom.

How much of this should have been interpreted? Analytic interpretation has long been concerned with making the unconscious conscious, generating self-consciousness or heightened self-awareness. But interpretations can also generate self-consciousness in the less desirable sense of awkwardness and self-preoccupation. Part of what was healing about Becky's experiences with me prior to the impactful interpretation was, I believe, precisely that they had an erotic dimension to them, a shared pleasure that was accepted between us and unremarked upon. There are, as we know, erotic dimensions in many intimate interactions. What went wrong with Becky's father was not their presence, but that they were split off from the fuller context of their relationship and exploited for the father's revenge against his wife. The shared (Mode 2) affect between Becky and me was gathered up into forms of interaction: (Mode 1) conversational patterns of deepening mutual interest; (Mode 3) experiential self-other configurations entailing a potent, exciting, and excited version of herself; and a (Mode 4) sense of intersubjective recognition of her own originality and self-expression.

These prior experiences in her interactions with me allowed Becky to use the interpretation of her omnipotence. In effect, I was inviting her to give up an illusory form of control over her experience, including her experience with me. In order to do so, she needed to feel that allowing affective sparks (and later, the interpretation itself) to play uncontrolled in the space between us would not result in her being abandoned, crushed, or controlled in ways she had felt as a child.

THE ANALYST'S CHOICES

What the analyst provides is a deeply personal engagement with the patient out of which both new understandings and new interpersonal and intrapsychic experiences emerge. Because of the relational density between analysand and analyst, there are many complex considerations that bear on how the analyst might most usefully proceed at any point in the process. Among the most important judgments the analyst has to make are those concerning what he *says* about what he *feels* and *does*.

The complexity of these judgments has sometimes been missed. Beginning candidates, in particular, sometimes develop the impression that the analyst's job is either to say almost nothing or else to disclose whatever it is he finds himself feeling and thinking about the patient. The multilevel framework I am proposing might be helpful not only in sorting out different interactive strands, but also in thinking through some of the choices about what to say and what not to say, which are a perpetual feature of analytic work.

The density of the episodes from my work with both Charles and Becky derives partly from the relationship between affect and speech in complex interpersonal contexts. At a particular point in the relationship between Charles and Sarah, not speaking about their feelings for each other seemed to present an obstacle to the deepening of the relationship between them. In the discussions of her thwarted writing projects between Becky and me, not speaking of the affective, mutually seductive features of our interaction seemed to open up a space within which certain feelings could develop more safely. What general interpersonal and technical conclusions might be drawn from this comparison? None at all!

One of the implications of the organizational framework I am proposing is that the relationships among affect, behavior, and language are enormously complex and contextual. The conventional pressure to say "I love you" often enough has a coercive, deadening impact on relationships. What was crucial for Charles was to decide whether or not he wanted to enhance the vitality of his relationship with Sarah; if he did, he needed to find a way, with or without language, to do so. And there are many situations in which it is enlivening for the analyst to express his feelings vis-à-vis the patient, or to put into words, through interpretations, his sense of what is transpiring between them. What seemed crucial for me at this point with Becky was to continually reflect upon the ways in which my responses to her situation repeated the earlier relational patterns of her childhood and then to find ways, with or without language, to participate with her in opening up new and more vital possibilities.

What is necessary is not the establishment of behavioral guidelines on the order of "interpret" or "do not interpret," but, rather, the development of conceptual guidelines to help clinicians think through the ongoing implications of whatever choices they make.

The wide array of relational concepts entering the analytic literature of recent years has considerable promise. What seems important at this point is to find ways of critically integrating different contributions to discover convergences and highlight differences, both with regard to human relationships in general and with respect to the always unique features of particular analytic situations.

CHAPTER 4

ATTACHMENT THEORY AND RELATIONALITY

Psychoanalysis has been struggling with the problems involved in addressing and understanding human relationality since the middle decades of the 20th century. The most important relational theorists were Harry Stack Sullivan, W. R. D. Fairbairn, Donald Winnicott, John Bowlby, and Hans Loewald. Because mainstream psychoanalysis was so solidly occupied, both ideologically and politically, by Freudian-Kleinian drive theory, each of these theorists was consigned to marginality during the years in which their major contributions were introduced and, in some cases, for their lifetimes. Sullivan never even tried to become part of the psychoanalytic community, and grouped his contributions during the 1930s and 1940s under the rubric of "interpersonal psychiatry." It was only later, through the efforts of Clara Thompson, that Sullivan's interpersonal point of view was blended together with Erich Fromm's "humanistic psychoanalysis" and Sandor Ferenczi's revolutionary clinical innovations to form an interpersonal school of psychoanalysis. For many decades, interpersonal psychoanalysts were considered by the mainstream to be "not psychoanalysts" at all. It has only been in the last ten years or so in the United States, as the mainstream itself has turned in the direction of relationality and interaction, that the contributions of Sullivan and his intellectual descendents have come to be acknowledged.

Fairbairn suffered a similar fate. His important contributions of the 1940s and early 1950s remained almost completely unrecognized until Harry Guntrip began to make them more accessible in the very different climate of the 1970s. In a review of Fairbairn's book *Psychoanalytic Studies of the Personality*, Winnicott and Khan (1953) put the central issue bluntly. Fairbairn, they suggest, asks us to choose between his theory and Freud's. They chose Freud's. Placing rationality at the center of motivation, development, and psychodynamics, in the way Fairbairn did, was regarded as obliterating what was most central to Freudian psychoanalysis — its foundation in drive theory.

Winnicott and Loewald had different fates. Winnicott was able to remain visible and influential within British psychoanalysis, and Loewald remained a respected and frequently cited figure within American psychoanalysis. I believe that what made this possible in both cases was obfuscation. Winnicott tended to retain classical terminology, even though his use and recontextualization of the terms radically changed their meanings. Further, he introduced his innovations in connection with the presumably severe pathology of false self disorders, as if not to challenge the received wisdom regarding neurosis, the traditional domain of classical psychoanalytic theorizing. Only gradually did it became apparent that Winnicott was introducing less an extension of traditional ideas into a new area than an alternative theory of mind.

Loewald, like Winnicott, retained traditional terminology, but unlike Winnicott, as we noted in chapters 1 and 2, Loewald spent a great deal of time explicitly redefining the terms. What made Loewald palatable to traditionalists was that his redefinitions were so talmudic and complex, his understanding so radical and visionary, that the revolutionary implications of his contributions were simply missed (Cooper, 1988).

BOWLBY AND THE PSYCHOANALYSIS OF HIS DAY

James Grotstein (1990) has suggested that the virtual expulsion of John Bowlby from psychoanalysis was "one of the most dreadful, shameful and regrettable chapters in the history of psychoanalysis" (p. 26). Several factors contributed to getting Bowlby into so much trouble. Probably most important among them was his clarity. Sullivan was a tortured, blocked writer. Fairbairn was tedious and difficult. Winnicott was poetic and elusive. Loewald was extremely subtle and often obscure. But Bowlby wrote with lucidity and power. To quote the conclusion of the third volume of his trilogy on attachment

(1980), "Intimate attachments to other human beings are the hub around which a person's life revolves, not only when he is an infant or a toddler or a school child but throughout his adolescence and his years of maturity as well, and on into old age" (p. 442). It was amply apparent from the very beginning and throughout that Bowlby (1960, 1969, 1973, 1980) regarded his contributions as a direct challenge to some of the basic principles of Freudian theory, and he had data on children in the real world to back up the challenge. He identified himself very much as a scientist, offering testable hypotheses, and his links with other scientists, especially the ethologists of his day, made his position extremely persuasive.[1] For the psychoanalytic establishment of Bowlby's time, all this was simply too much to bear.

But there was another issue that contributed to creating the broad schism between Bowlby's attachment theory and psychoanalysis. The language of psychoanalysis is psychodynamics. Freud early on defined psychodynamics, drawing as was his custom on the physics of his day, in terms of "forces" in the mind, specifically instinctually based impulsive forces and mental defenses against them. Just as physicists have changed greatly from Freud's day to ours in their understanding of material forces, so have the ways psychoanalysts understand and talk about psychodynamics. With the fading of drive metapsychology and the energic model, psychoanalysts today talk more about internal objects, self-states, representations, and internal relations among selves and objects. But the signature feature of psychoanalysis and its language remains its focus on internality, the description of conscious and unconscious subjective states.

Bowlby, like Sullivan, had a more behavioral sensibility. Neither was a behaviorist in the strict sense of the term, but both were much more interested than the typical psychoanalyst in what actually goes on between people in the real world. The roots of this sensibiility for Sullivan were in philosophical pragmatism, which dominated the American social science of his day. There is no use talking about what you can't see or measure operationally, Sullivan believed. In trying to understand "human difficulties in living" it is much more economical, conceptually speaking, to study what we have termed Mode 1 interactions — what people actually do with each other. The roots of this sensibility for Bowlby were in the neighboring discipline of ethology, which provided powerful explanatory concepts for understanding what Bowlby had been observing in children's reactions to separation and loss.

No single author has had nearly as much impact on Western intellectual history of the past 150 years, including the history of psychoanalytic ideas, as Charles Darwin. Both Freud and Bowlby were extremely involved with Darwin's contribution, but their Darwins were very different. Freud's Darwin was part of the first wave of reaction to the extraordinary implications of the theory of evolution; one of Freud's projects was to work out the implications for human psychology of Darwin's demonstration of the continuity between so-called lower and so-called higher forms of animal life. Freud's fascination with primitivism has a recurrent thematic consistency throughout his writings. Indeed, Freud's structural model of the psyche is a recreation, on a microcosmic level, of Darwin's sweeping macrocosmic account of the evolution of species: the lower level, primitive energy of the id is transformed by the reality-oriented ego into higher level, aim-inhibited resources for activities consistent with the cultural values of the superego. Ontogeny recapitulates phylogeny.

Bowlby draws on a different Darwin.[2] Like Heinz Hartmann, Bowlby was most interested in what Darwin taught about animal adaptation to environmental conditions and niches. In the second volume of his attachment trilogy, Bowlby (1973) refers to Freud as pre-Darwinian, because he did not grasp the importance of the principle of "natural selection" in Darwin's theory of the evolution of species. Bowlby, like Darwin, was interested in what animals do to maximize their chances for survival. In the principles of ethology he found tools for conceptualizing the concerns he had developed in his early work with autistic children and his study of childhood health and pathology for the World Health Organization. Whereas Freud's Darwin lent himself to the study of internality and unconscious, primitive states, Bowlby's Darwin lent himself to a behavioral analysis of what small children and mothers actually *do* with each other.

Slade (1998) has elegantly summarized the key notions running throughout Bowlby's work:

(a) that the child is born with a predisposition to become attached to his caregivers, (b) that the child will organize his behavior and thinking in order to maintain these attachment relationships, which are key to his psychological and physical survival, (c) that the child will often maintain such relationships at great cost to his own functioning, and (d) the distortions in feeling and thinking that stem from early disturbances in attachment occur most often in response to the parents' inability to meet the child's needs for comfort, security, and emotional reassurance [p. 3].

The advantage of this largely behavioral emphasis has been that Bowlby's ideas have been applied, with extraordinary effectiveness, to the empirical research tradition that Mary Ainsworth and Mary Main have done so much to develop. The disadvantage of Bowlby's behavioral emphasis has been the relative underdevelopment of psychodynamic dimensions (Modes 2, 3, and 4), which has made the bridge to mainstream psychoanalysis more difficult. As Holmes (1996, p. xiv) has recently pointed out, attachment theory has been more productively applied to research than to clinical work.

Bowlby's concept of "working models" was an early, abstract, undeveloped effort to depict the psychodynamic residues of the vicissitudes of attachment experiences. Main (1995) has noted a recent "relational turn" by attachment theorists, in their efforts to depict those internal residues. This development within the attachment tradition, together with the turn toward relationality in the psychoanalytic tradition, makes this a particularly appropriate time to explore the convergence between these quasi-independent lines of theory making.

BOWLBY AND THE PSYCHOANALYSIS OF OUR DAY

Some of the conceptual divergences that have divided the psychoanalytic and attachment traditions were historical artifacts that have been rendered obsolete by recent developments. The psychoanalysis that Bowlby rejected privileged fantasy over actuality, deriving from

Freud's own reversal, in 1897, of his original seduction theory. Before 1897, Freud believed that actual events, childhood sexual seductions, were the cause of neurosis. After 1897, Freud believed that actual abuse sometimes happened and was important, but that the core of neurosis lay in childhood sexual fantasies. Unconscious fantasy became the central concern of psychoanalysis ever since.

Bowlby always seemed to regard the choice between privileging "real events" versus "fantasy" as a key fork in the road separating attachment theory from psychoanalysis. British psychoanalysis has been dominated by Kleinian theory, in which actual family interactions are regarded largely as the medium upon which the child's primitive fantasies are projected. He noted in an interview late in his life, "I was told in no uncertain terms that it was not an analyst's job to pay attention to real life events — as explicit as that" (Hunter, 1991, p. 173). Bowlby (personal communication) recalled a meeting of the British Society during his early years in training in which he stood up and emphatically made the point, "But there *is* such a thing as a *bad* mother!"

Thus, fantasy became a problem for Bowlby because in his day fantasy, in its link with drive theory, signified distorted, primal patterns that were imposed on real life. Bowlby, by contrast, had become increasingly convinced that actual life — real mothers and real events — had a determinative influence on development.

The distinction between fantasy and reality, however, is not drawn so sharply in current psychoanalytic theorizing. Some of the more innovative psychoanalytic authors do not link fantasy with drives, but with imagination. In this view, which began with Winnicott and, as we noted in chapter 1, was significantly developed by Loewald, reality is encountered, inevitably, *through* imagination and fantasy. Fantasy and actuality are not alternatives; they interpenetrate and potentially enrich one another.

On the other side of the psychoanalysis-attachment theory divide, recent developments by attachment researchers and theorists have produced some remarkable data and concepts of great interest to psychoanalysts. Mary Ainsworth operationalized Bowlby's concept of attachment by developing the extraordinarily productive, controlled setting she called the "strange situation," empirically demonstrating a close relationship between varying parental responsiveness in the home and different kinds of attachment styles manifested in a novel circumstance of controlled separation from the mother.

Ainsworth's construction of the setting of the "strange situation" was one of the places where Bowlby's immersion in ethology had a direct and fertile impact (John Kerr, personal communication). Ethologists studying flocks of geese on a lake found themselves with long-standing patterns of dominance already established and therefore operating invisibly. Konrad Lorenz developed a strategy for enticing the flock to a new pond, where the power hierarchies would need to be reestablished. Kerr points out that in studying small children at home, Bowlby and Ainsworth encountered the same problem. Is the child playing comfortably, secure about his mother's presence in the next room, or is he avoiding her? So the strange situation operates like the new pond, where the child's security vis-à-vis the mother is challenged and characteristic patterns are displayed. Many subsequent experiments have demonstrated the enormous predictive value of the attachment style displayed by one-year-olds in the strange situation in relation to a variety of measures of subsequent cognitive, emotional, and social development as the children grow older.

More recently, Main (1995) and her collaborators have studied attachment phenomena across generations, exploring the relationship between a parent's early attachment experiences and his or her infant's attachment status measured by the strange situation. They developed the "Adult Attachment Interview" to determine retrospectively the nature of the parent's own early attachment experiences, assuming that the better the experiences of the parent, the more secure the parent, the more securely attached the child would be. But their results were quite unexpected. What was important was not whether the parent had been deprived or nurtured as a child, but the degree of coherence versus incoherence in the parent's subsequent memory of her childhood. What was crucial was not so much the content of what had happened, the actual events and behaviors, but the narrative organization through which the past had been processed. This emphasis in recent conceptualizations of attachment bears close resemblance to the importance in recent psychoanalytic theorizing of the themes of hermeneutics, constructivism, and narrativity (see, for example, Schafer, 1992).

The evocative recent explorations by Peter Fonagy and his collaborators (Fonagy et al., 1992, 1995; Fonagy and Target, 1996, 1998) of
"reflective self-function" and "mentalization" as key processes
through which secure attachment is mediated have opened up another bridge between the attachment tradition and psychoanalytic
developmental theory. As Slade (1997) has put it, "what Main and
Fonagy specifically alert us to is listening for coherence, for the capacity to reflect upon and make sense of internal experience, and to listen
for *incoherence,* of meaninglessness, of disorganization, and of disintegration, for moments when meaning cannot be made" (p. 15).

In addition to the polarization of internal-external, fantasy reality
in the psychoanalysis of his day, Bowlby struggled with other dichotomies that have been transcended in the psychoanalysis of our
day, particularly within contempoary relational thinking: the contrast between the intrapsychic versus the interpersonal, and the
location of the therapeutic agent in insight versus relationship. Mace
and Margison (1997) noted that there has been a tension within the
attachment literature between a "cognitive effort towards understanding of the unsatisfactory working model, and a fundamental
attempt to offer recapitulation through a positive attachment experience" (p. 213). Current relational authors tend to regard the analyst's
interpretive understanding as part of the particularly analytic form
of positive attachment experience and, conversely, the kind of attachment experience the analyst offers as containing interpretive and
metainterpretive dimensions. In short, what has happened since
Bowlby introduced his revolutionary attachment theory has been the
introduction and elaboration of the other relational perspectives,
centered around affect permeability, self and object configurations,
and intersubjectivity, that we have located, along with attachment,
within the interactional hierarchy. These developments suggest that
this is a particularly timely moment to explore convergences.

THE INNER WORLD OF LOSS

Connie had the kind of early experiences for which attachment theory
seems custom-designed; she had suffered an early, catastrophic loss
of her mother when she was five years old. She had had a quite
successful earlier experience in psychotherapy that ended about ten

years before she came to see me. In many ways, both Connie's earlier therapy and her work with me were largely concerned with the implications of her early loss. In our work, however, various other psychodynamic facets emerged that I find useful to conceptualize in terms of the contributions of Fairbairn, Winnicott, Loewald, and interpersonal psychoanalysis. Therefore, this work lends itself to an exercise in juxtaposing and playing with Bowlby's concepts together with those of other psychoanalytic authors. I don't want to suggest that all these theories are congruent and integratable at all points. Winnicott, for example, locates the core of the individual in a solitary privacy, which is quite different from the more interactive self of Loewald and Sullivan. But these authors all have illuminated crucial features of relationality that, taken together, have generated a powerful and compelling account of human interaction.

Connie returned for treatment in her mid 40s for two reasons. First, the chronic sadness that had haunted her her whole life, which had been somewhat alleviated by psychotherapy in her 30s, had returned. Her mother had died suddenly in a car accident when she was five years old. In her first therapy it had become clear that her persistent sense of sadness and episodic tearfulness were connected with an aborted mourning for her mother that had never been able to take place. Her father had felt that the loss of their mother was just too painful for Connie and her older brother to speak about, so she was never mentioned throughout Connie's childhood. In her earlier therapy, she began to speak about and feel her loss directly for the first time. She remembered finding a picture of her mother hidden away in a closet when she was a child. She recalled going into the closet and searching that picture longingly, trying to stir up memories of the mother who had quickly faded from her experience. That therapy was very important to her; it provided an opportunity for a mourning process that had never been allowed to happen, and it placed her sadness in a context of meaning. But considerable sadness remained, and it increased in severity when she married in her late 30s and had a son, who himself was now five years old. This boy, not suprisingly but very disturbingly to her, had extremely intense separation problems. She knew this must have something to do with the loss of her mother at the same age he was now, and she was concerned about imposing on him the tragedy of her own early life.

The second reason Connie sought another analytic treatment was that she had always felt there was something different about her, something other people had that she lacked. They seemed to have a "self," it appeared, some much more grounded sense of who they are. Even though she was objectively an extremely accomplished and creative person, she felt she lacked that inner sense. She knew that lack had something to do with the loss of her mother and the "hole" she felt in her experience ever since. She imagined that one of the things a mother does for a child is to help him recognize who he is, what he is like, and she tried especially hard to do that with her own son. But would it ever be possible to find that missing experience for herself?

One of the first things that became apparent in our work was that Connie's early loss went way beyond the loss of her mother. Her father felt completely overwhelmed by the death of his wife and his responsibility for his two young children. He decided the only possible plan was to send them both to boarding school. The older brother went off to a miliary school and Connie went off to an orphanage-boarding school run by nuns, several hundred miles from her home. The nuns took good care of her, but it was an almost completely anonymous life. She lived in a dormitory with other girls; her bed was like all the other beds, with all signs of distinct and distinguishing characteristics disallowed. One of her most vivid visceral memories of the nuns was the starched bibs they wore, betraying nothing of warm breasts or body underneath. Connie would return home to be with her father on weekends. She felt extremely grateful that he would come to pick her up each weekend, because there were other girls who were orphaned and had nobody. She wrote to her father every day, telling him she loved him, so as to remind him not to forget about her. It was only after seven years that her father felt the children were old enough to return home on a regular basis. On the weekends with her father, and in living with him after the children returned home, Connie experienced her father as extremely overtaxed and brittle. It seemed desperately important never to burden him with her own needs, as if the fragile elements of a home that were provided could instantly cave in. So, Connie lost more than her mother at age five; in effect, she lost her whole world.

It is, of course, impossible to capture the complex texture of an analytic process in writing. But I would like to pull out several themes and incidents from our work to illustrate the ways in which attachment issues and problems play out on different levels of relationality. Taken together, they provide a rich conceptual framework for thinking about the interactive matrix that constitutes the psychoanalytic process.

ATTACHMENT AND (MODE 2) PERMEABILITY OF BOUNDARIES OF INTIMACY

During a stretch of several weeks when her son's separation problems had been quite acute, Connie began to describe, somewhat shamefully, her sense that her son was "part of me." This, of course, is not what enlightened parents are supposed to think. But we explored some ways in which this was in fact her reality. She described her experience of watching him play with his classmates. She couldn't take her eyes off him. It was as if he were endlessly fascinating. I knew something about what she was describing from experiences with my own children, but her feelings seemed to be more intense and pervasive. So, I asked her to see if she could get at the feelings connected with the sense that "he is part of me."

Connie remembered her absorption in her pregnancy when, in a quite literal sense, her son *was* part of her. She remembered the strangeness of the separation that constituted his birth; he still felt part of her, although no longer literally part of her. She then associated to her memories that in losing her mother she had lost a "part" of herself. In fact, she'd felt an absence, a kind of hole, in herself ever since that time, as if a part of her had disappeared and never returned. She'd felt that perhaps in becoming a mother, she could refind her mother once again. I suggested that when she lost her mother she had also lost a version of herself, and that her fascination with her son was partly a fascination with a childhood of which she herself had been robbed. In watching him, she was also watching for lost parts of herself and for the lost mother who had never seen them.

How would we want to characterize Connie's experience of her son as "part of me." Is this an illusion? Is it a primitive fantasy? Is it a break in reality-testing? It is here that I find helpful Loewald's notion that we organize our experience on different levels simultaneously. As we noted earlier, Loewald depicts a "primary process" organized around a primal density of experience, in which dichotomies like self-other, past-present, inner-outer do not exist, and a "secondary process" in which the customary categories of conventional, adaptive living apply. Loewald's concerns are close to Winnicott's in the latter's descriptions of transitional phenomena, but in his final work, as we noted in chapter 1, Loewald (1988) stressed what is a very important difference from Winnicott. The latter regards the early subjective experiences of the child, including transitional experience, as suffused with omnipotence and illusion. Loewald regards many primary process experiences, particularly those of undifferentiation between self and others, as not illusions at all. For Loewald, primary process and secondary process constitute alternative and equally valid, equally "real" forms of organizing experience. The task of psychoanalysis is not a transformation of primary process into secondary process, not a removal of fantasy and distortion, but an opening up of the severed, potentially enriching links *between* fantasy and actuality.

Thus, Connie's experience of her son as "part of me" might be understood as a reality of a different sort than the conventional one we generally inhabit. Connie's early catastrophic loss seems to have been experienced not only as the loss of an other, but as the loss of an other, a self, a world, all jumbled up together. Her pregnancy filled, temporarily, the hole left by that loss, and her son came to signify for her parts of herself that were there and parts of herself she experienced only as absences. He, in turn, must have come to experience her losses and terror of separation as his own. According to Loewald, it is a mistake to understand these experiences as fantasied distortions of reality due to pathological, aborted mourning. Rather, they are pieces of reality. On a primary process level, we are not separate from our significant others; in intense emotional experiences, we cocreate events and share resonating emotions that are not neatly assignable to discrete categories like self-other and inner-outer. Adding Mode 2 considerations of affective permeability to Bowlby's work, we might speculate that the residue of attachment experiences, both early on and through later life, includes not simply cognitive working models of the interpersonal world, but affective states of undifferentiated connection with attachment figures, organized around both positive affects, like euphoria or soothing calm, and negative affects, like depression, anxiety, or terror. In this view, what Connie needs to accomplish in psychoanalysis is not a neat separation from her mother and her son, but a greater capacity to contain varied experiences of both union with and differentiation from them.

ATTACHMENT AND THE (MODE 3) STRUCTURALIZATION OF THE SELF WITH OTHERS

In speaking about the "hole" left by her mother's death, Connie came to elaborate the ways in which she felt different from other people. As we returned to this theme repeatedly, in its many different variations, it became increasingly apparent the extent to which the loss of her mother and its impact on her life had become the way in which Connie had come to define herself, to distinguish herself from others. Her sadness, even though anguishing, had, she feared, become her destiny. She couldn't remember her mother; all she had was the hole rent in the fabric of her experience that her mother's disappearance had left behind.

Main (1995) notes the shift from the early notion that disturbances in mothering generate poorly or weakly attached children to the understanding, more compatible with Fairbairn's notion of attachment to "bad" objects, that children inevitably become powerfully attached to whatever is availble. "Quantitative terms (such as 'strongly' or 'weakly' attached) are not used in describing differences among individuals. . . . Infants who have become attached to maltreating or simply insensitive attachment figures are presumed no 'less' attached than others, and virtually all infants become attached" (pp. 411–412). In this sense, rather than distinguishing between secure and insecure attachments, we might distinguish between attachments to secure and insecure or absent objects. For Connie, her mother's absence created a powerful presence; her attachment to that absence served as a central, defining feature of her sense of self. Her continual unconscious mourning for her mother served as a perpetual object tie linking Connie to her mother.

This theme resurfaced throughout her life in ways that I found surprising and fascinating. One session she began talking about a new book she was finding captivating about groups of climbers on Mt. Everest. As we explored its power for her, she began to speak of "extreme situations," like climbing Everest, as something she often fantasized about and also had sought out in some wilderness travel. Her visit to the tundra in Alaska had been a high point in her life. There was something about the self-state generated amid the bleakness of the tundra landscape, the gripping feeling of the enormity of the world and her own smallness that, paradoxically, generated a sense of serenity and security she found so hard to come by. Such a world seemed "unforgiving," she said, and it was that very quality she found reassuring. Similarly, in the long-distance running and swimming she spent a lot of time doing, she felt closest to contacting that sense of self she found so elusive in other circumstances. As she drove herself past pain, she felt she had some defining sense of who she was, what sort of a person she could be.

One could think of these experiences in terms of guilt and masochism. Did Connie feel somehow responsible for her mother's death? Was the "unforgiving" quality of bleakness and pain a self-punishment for what she felt had been her crime? But along Fairbairnian lines, it also seemed as if the bleakness and enormity of the wilderness and her ability to survive and transcend pain evoked something of the aching emptiness of her losses and the "unforgiving" world of the school in which she found herself and had survived. In the absence of a secure attachment figure, the bleakness and pain itself had become a point of reference for self-recognition.

In her current life, Connie spends a lot of time thinking about what constitutes a "home" and how to provide a home for her son. In discussing these issues, at one point that I found particularly poignant she said she always had very powerful feelings associated with the particular sound of a screen door closing. In fact, she loved that sound so much that she had once tried to have a custom-made, miniature screen door built that she could keep on her desk. Her associations led to the feeling, as a kid, of going out the back door of her house into the backyard and the rest of the world, and feeling the solidity of the house behind her that the sound of the door conveyed to her. It was as if that sound was an anchor, a point of attachment.

As we have noted, Bowlby's behavioral-ethological contributions on attachment were accompanied by an account of "working
models," which, he suggested, were the residue of attachment experiences. The cognitive emphasis in the notion of models is suple-
mented and enriched by considering the sorts of (Mode 3) self-other
configurations that result from different sorts of attachment experiences. Thus, the centrality of Connie's attachment to her mother's
absence not only provided a conceptual map or model of what she
might expect in the world, but constituted one of the major forms
through which she became a self with others, became *her*self. Some
of Winnicott's concepts shed additional light on the ways in which
the self becomes structuralized through interactions with others and,
in the absence of certain parental provisions, through self-structures
playing the role of the other.

Connie considered the sadness that had been a constant accompaniment of her life since her early childhood to be connected with the
loss of her mother and the subsequent loss of mothering throughout
her childhood. The first therapy had made that sadness more vivid
and meaningful, but had not helped her free herself of it. There were
times during that work that she felt almost paralyzed by her feelings.
She had a deep fear of coming back for more analytic work, because
she experienced her mournful sadness as a bottomless pit. She hoped
our work would help free her of it, but she feared that even more
painful losses would be stirred up.

After a while I began to feel that there was something in the way
Connie organized her current experiences that contributed to regenerating her sadness, that her feelings reflected something she was
giving up in the present as much as something she had lost in the
past. Somehow, probably because it is one of *my* favorite subjects, we
had gotten into speaking about her approach to food and eating. She
tended to be extremely health conscious, with a focus on eating salads
and vegetables. She allowed herself one bag of M&M's each after-
noon, however. I have always disliked M&M's, so I became intrigued
with the specificity of that choice. She liked M&M's partly because
each bit of chocolate was embedded in a hard shell; it was "modular,"
she said. Now I like my chocolate accompanied by a sense of limitless
self-indulgence. I wondered whether she ever ate Milky-Ways. Of
course she had tried them, but the thing about Milky-Ways was

precisely that their richness and size could easily make you feel sick and regretful after a while. Connie reflected on the way in which the kind of supervisory care that she provided for her son's eating had been lost for her with the death of her mother. There *was* nobody to watch out for the health implications, short- and long-term, of what she ate. She learned early on to do that for herself. She would start with what seemed conscientious and sensible and then let herself desire what was feasible. I compared that silently with my own experience, which moves in the other direction, from an initial impulse of limitless desire to regretful considerations connected with having a mortal body in the real world. I mused with Connie about the implications of her never having had the experience, at least within memory, of not having to worry about real considerations of health and safety, of being able to give oneself over to impulses of sheer desire and pleasure, taking for granted that someone else would be watching over. We began to feel that her sadness was in part an ongoing present accompaniment of the sensible and conscientious approach to living that had enabled her to survive.

I began to realize that we were dealing with issues of the sort that Winnicott had described in his exploration of the ways in which personal meaning and a sense of self are generated. "True self" experience, in Winnicott's terms, begins with a "spontaneous gesture" that emerges from a core of subjective omnipotence; spontaneous gestures are, in the beginning, actualized by the "good-enough mother" and thereby consolidated into a sense of oneself as good and real. Because Connie had lost that parental provision precipitously, she had to take over that caretaking role for herself. The consequence was not so much a sense of "falseness," in Winnicott's terms, but a chronic sense of sadness and of something missing.

We began to realize that Connie's approach to chocolate was prototypical of her way of organizing much of her experience, including personal relationships. She would figure out what was possible to have, and then let herself want things within those borders. The area of her life in which considerable sadness was generated through this approach was with her husband, who was quite self-absorbed. Although he actually seemed to have a deep emotional commitment to her, if not pushed, he could easily convey the impression that he was not available for much intimacy. And especially in her experience with her father, Connie had learned that a seamless adaptation to what was available, not pushing, was the way to survive.

Bowlby and Ainsworth pointed to the provision in secure attachment of a safe base for an exploration of the world. This aspect of the work with Connie suggests that another experience that secure attachment provides is the safety to explore not just the external world, but the internal world of personal preferences, desires, and impulses, what Winnicott (1960) called "spontaneous gestures." When the safety that a dependable attachment figure provides is missing, the child herself tends precociously to fill in the missing parental function (Winnicott's "care-taker self") and opportunities for a worry-free surrender to one's own experience is foreclosed (see also Ghent, 1992, on surrender).

ATTACHMENT AND (MODE 4) INTERSUBJECTIVITY

Among the most radical implications of Sullivan's (1953) concept of the interpersonal field was the notion that mind is not something each of us carries around inside our skulls, in control over how much to reveal or conceal of it to others, but that mind is transpersonal and contextual. Mind emerges in interactions with other minds. No matter how much of an observer the analyst tries to be, Sullivan was suggesting, he is also inevitably a participant. Fromm (1994), in his "Humanistic Psychoanalysis," added to Sullivan's concept of the interpersonal field an emphasis on the analytic situation as a kind of existential encounter. No matter what else might be going on, Fromm believed, the patient comes to the analyst for honest talk, for frank engagement. These early concepts of Sullivan and Fromm were developed by subsequent interpersonal theorists into an approach to the analytic process that emphasizes the here-and-now relationship between the two participants. Whereas theorists within the British independent group, like Fairbairn, Winnicott, and Balint, wrote about the analytic relationship in terms of missing parental provisions and functions, the interpersonalists wrote about the analytic relationship in less developmental, more intersubjective terms. In the contributions of Levenson (1972, 1983), in particular, the analyst is portrayed as inevitably embedded within the transference-countertransference mix. And, as we noted in chapter 3, the nature and developmental trajectory of intersubjectivity has been explored in the contributions of Jessica Benjamin and others.

With this background in mind, consider several important points in the evolution of the analytic relationship that Connie and I coconstructed, in which, I believe, the expansion of the qualities of intersubjectivity between us provided her with different sorts of attachment experiences than her early life had allowed.

Despite my suggestion that a greater frequency would be preferrable, Connie began our work on a once-per-week basis, which was more than enough for her, thank you. She was extremely wary of the feelings that might be unleashed, and was concerned about the dangers of being in therapy for the rest of her life.

Connie used the time very conscientiously and productively from the start. She was a keen and thoughtful observer of her own experience. I liked her very much and enjoyed talking with her. I soon found the once-a-week frequency depriving. I found myself wanting more of her, and, upon reflection, realized that I was feeling something like *her* childhood feelings of longing in relation to her father's weekly visits. But it wasn't only the frequency that seemed rigidly controlled. Any questions about feelings she might be having in relation to me were met with incredulity. Why would she have feelings about me? This was a strictly professional relationship, after all. There was clearly something in this of her experiences with the nuns. Any personal feelings between us would be inappropriate and would likely end up in painful longing. She said this in a manner that made me feel as if my even entertaining the idea that we might actually have feelings about each other was a sign of immaturity and perverse silliness on my part. So I stayed at my assigned distance and waited.[3]

A couple of months into the work, Connie surprised me by beginning a session in considerable distress. How did this therapy work? she wanted to know. She felt there was something terribly impersonal about the way I greeted her in the waiting room, without even saying her name, right after the previous, probably equally anonymous patient had left. At first I felt a little stung by this accusation, particularly because I had been struggling myself with what felt to me to be a distance imposed by her. I began to wonder if I had not unconsciously retaliated by toning down my emotional reactions to her at the beginning and ending of our sessions. I do tend sometimes to be rather businesslike. And my customary way of greeting patients was to acknowledge their presence with a "hello" and invite them into my office without mentioning their names. We explored Connie's experience of these interactions, but she was still angry. I explained that it was just not my customary style to mention people's names when I met them, either inside or outside the therapy setting. She felt that what she experienced as the anonymity of my manner was intolerable, and that unless I would sometimes mention her name, she would be unable to continue. We agreed that it would not make sense for me to do this mechanically, but that I would try to find a way that was genuine for me. And I did. I actually found that I enjoyed saying her name. And her responses to my greetings were warmer than they had been before. I realized that there *was* something a bit pressured about my "let's get down to work" attitude. I even began to change my manner of greeting and parting from other patients. It seemed to me that Connie and I were working something out related to distance and intimacy, presence and loss, that was not unrelated to her early traumas and deprivations, but that was happening in a very lively way between us now. A couple of months following our newly fashioned manner of greeting and parting, Connie said she felt she had too much to talk about in one weekly session, and she began to come twice a week.

The work continued to go well, focusing on recurrent patterns in different areas of her life. She reported feeling better, somehow, less chronically sad and more grounded in a sense of who she is. We would periodically speak about her sense of oddness about our sessions, how unrelated they seemed to the rest of her life. Shortly after leaving, she often had trouble remembering what we had spoken of, and she almost seemed suprised to find herself there again at the beginning of sessions. We looked at her struggles with keeping the connection with me alive from many different angles.

About a year into the work, Connie reported for several weeks a strong feeling of not wanting to come for sessions. We were both puzzled by these feelings, but felt we would come to learn more about them as we went along. She then reported a dream in which she got into a taxi; her destination was a very desolate, windy street. The driver was an Indian or Pakistani with a turban, who, she slowly realized, was angry, threatening, and probably dangerous. She was considering how she would get out of the taxi when the dream ended.

Her associations to the street were to a childhood friend who had become schizophrenic and lived in a halfway house on the edge of the city in which they had grown up, by the water. It was indeed a very windy place. Then there was my street, which is also pretty windy. We played with the sense of me as unknown, exotic, strange, threatening, perhaps dangerous. She felt that the dream reflected a sense that the work with me had become, somewhat suprisingly, important to her, and that she wasn't sure where that would leave her. We spoke of her need to keep me separated from the rest of her life—out at the end of the earth. There was something about that splitting that kept me safe for her to touch base with and leave, and also kept the rest of her life safe for her to handle on her own. But her locating me out on the periphery of her world also made me foreign, distant, and unknown.

About a week later she reported a powerful experience with her husband, or, more accurately, in her feelings toward her husband. Their relationship was quite caring and mutually supportive in times of crisis, but, in many respects, quite distant and cool in an ongoing way. We had been working, on and off, on the part she played in maintaining that distance. She had come to realize that she had long ago decided that her husband was simply unavailable to meet her emotional needs, and so she had stopped even being aware of having any such needs vis-à-vis him. Recently, she had become aware of wanting things from him and had tried, with varying degrees of success, to express those desires with him.

The experience she reported was of going to bed after he had already gone to sleep. She had the compelling thought that she might wake him to make love; it felt that such a gesture would constitute a forgiveness of her chronic grievances against him. She decided not to wake him and, as was her custom, simply went quietly to sleep beside him. We explored, among other things, her sense that to be close to him in one way would entail renouncing her right to her own needs in other ways.

In the next session, Connie reported a fight they had had. It was typical of their fights, but had a somewhat different ending. He had left a used tea bag in the sink. His untidiness had been a chronic issue between them. He had grown up in a wealthy family, with maids to clean up after him. They lived a comfortable but by no means luxurious life now, with no maids. Connie felt he continually left messes for her to clean up. They had made some progress — in early years the tea bag would have been left on the table. But she felt a deep sense of bitterness at what she felt was his taking her for granted. She expressed this to him, and he felt attacked, leading to counterattacks. He was effective at debate, and, traditionally, she would give in, apologizing for what seemed to be the inappropriate intensity of her anger. That surrender would leave her feeling demoralized and despairing. This time she defended her position without giving in, which was a considerable accomplishment. But she felt an aching sense that she would never feel taken into account as a person in the way she longed for.

I got interested in the way Connie presented her concerns to her husband, through the kind of "detailed inquiry" Sullivan (1954) wrote about extensively. (His methodology of finding out exactly "Who said what to whom?" can sometimes be very enlightening and might be considered to be a training in the kind of self-reflection recently studied by Fonagy and his collaborators.) By the time Connie opened up these discussions with her husband, she was already very angry, and his sense that he was being attacked seemed understandable to me. But what was really demoralizing to her was the sense that he operated as if she did not exist for him, as if she had no presence in his mind. And in the end, it was her chronic, pervasive sense of isolation that contributed to her perpetual sadness.

I did what I often do in this kind of situation: I tried to imagine another way to deal with the situation that might lead to a more constructive outcome (cf. Frank, 1999). I told her that it seemed to me that the issue was really not the power negotiation over who did what jobs, always an important issue within couples, but that she ended up feeling invisible to him, trapped in her familiar but sad solitude. I asked her what she thought might happen if she opened the discussion with him by explaining that she valued a feeling of connection with him, that his acting as if he were unaware of the impact of his behavior on her made her feel as if she had no place in his mind. The issue was not to control or criticize him, but to find a way for the two of them to feel mindful of and related to each other. Connie found herself amazed at the thought that she might broach these issues with him. She realized that the reason she would never have thought about approaching him in that way was it would imply that she actually had some ongoing emotional need for connection with him, and that certainly wasn't something of which she was ordinarily aware.

Suggesting alternative ways of handling interpersonal situations is not generally considered within the bounds of traditional analytic technique. But I sometimes find it very useful. The suggestions are almost never simply picked up on and used. That is not the point. What is invariably most interesting and useful are the patient's thoughts and feelings in reaction to my imaginary alternatives. They are really a kind of thought experiment.

Connie returned for the next session brimming with intense mixed feelings. She'd been thinking a great deal about the previous session. It was true that the sense of emotional connection to her husband, a sense that she had a presence in his mind, was very important to her, she now realized. To actively express that need seemed both exhilarating and frightening. She feared that anyone becoming aware of her needs for them would likely feel burdened and abandon her. And she had trouble imagining that she could actually give expression to such needs and still remain herself — such an act seemed so far from the self she had long recognized herself to be. While she felt excited at the prospect of exploring new possibilities, she nonetheless resented the fact that such cathartic feelings and exhilarating thoughts had emerged in her therapy, rather than in conversation with her husband. I kidded her about her fear of catharsis outside of marriage, and we laughed together about that. Sessions over the next several months primarily explored various facets of her relationship with her husband, in which she become more adept at locating and expressing her own needs, both for contact with him and freedom from his need of her. In one discussion, which was extraordinarily important to her, he had come out of his absorption in his own work to speak to her. Rather than make herself grudgingly available, as was her wont, Connie told him that at that moment, on Tuesday evening at

10:00, watching her favorite TV show was actually more important to her than being available to speak with him. Although seemingly trivial, this was an extremely precarious act of extraordinary personal freedom for her in their relationship. It seemed as if her increased ability to be aware of and to express her attachment to him also allowed Connie to begin to be able to establish her independence from him, without the paralyzing dread of losing him.

The concept of attachment has become increasingly refined in recent years; various kinds of attachments, with different qualities, have been delineated. Fonagy and Target (1998) have explored the ways in which secure attachment experiences result in a complex sense of intersubjectivity, in which one comes to a sense of oneself as an agentic subject through the experience of oneself in the mind of the other, and the other-as-agentic subject in one's own mind.

The major relational authors have contributed in different ways to our clinical understanding of different facets and implications of human relationality and attachment. Loewald's innovative theorizing suggests that the apparent separation between the subject who attaches and the object of attachment overlays a primary process level of organization in which self and other exist in various degrees of undifferentiation from each other. Loewald suggests that healthy object relations (and by implication, healthy attachments) consist not so much in a clear separation of self from others, but in a capacity to contain in dialectical tensions different mutually enriching forms of relatedness. Fairbairn explored the psychodynamics of attachments to physically or emotionally absent parenting figures, and the ways in which they become established as internal presences, devotion to which draws one away from new relationships. Winnicott illuminated the subtle ways in which secure attachment facilitates the development of a personal sense of self and the ways in which the absence of such parental functions adaptively forecloses such development. And finally, Sullivan, contemporary interpersonalists, and theorists of intersubjectivity have contributed to our understanding of the ways in which the vicissitudes of early attachment experiences play themselves out in current relationships, including the transference-countertransference relationship with the analyst.

At this point in the evolution of psychological ideas, attachment theory and psychoanalytic theory, rather than offering alternative pathways, offer the exciting possibility of a convergence that is mutually enriching.

CHAPTER 5

FAIRBAIRN'S OBJECT-SEEKING
Between Paradigms

One of the clearest lessons to be gleaned from the enormous body of Freud scholarship, which has become a field of intellectual history in its own right, is that major theoreticians can be read in many, many different ways. A second lesson is that it is probably a mistake to expect any great innovator to really grasp the revolution in which he or she is participating. Because they are standing in one worldview and struggling to give birth to another, they cannot possibly envision the full fruition of their efforts. Thus, Loewald (1980), Habermas (1968), and Lear (1990), each in his own way, argue that Freud only incompletely understood the revolution he himself was effecting. Ogden (1989) has argued that it is not only impossible to understand Melanie Klein's work without having read Freud, but that it is impossible to understand Freud without having first read Klein, because the work of Klein and others brought to life potentials that were only germinal in Freud's writings.

Fairbairn is a case in point. He too was a man of his time, operating with the conceptual and linguistic conventions that were the intellectual coin of his day. But Fairbairn was also a visionary, struggling with what he felt were basic problems with the psychoanalytic understanding of human experience in which he had been trained. Fairbairn is important for our purposes because he provided an early radical account of relationality that has come to be increasingly influential in recent decades. It is Fairbairn's concepts that have provided the most widely used terms for depicting Mode 3, or self-other, configurations. But there was no way for Fairbairn himself to have forseen the full implications of what he had wrought, and Fairbairn has been read and positioned in many different ways.

In this chapter I suggest a reading of Fairbairn that portrays him as struggling to move from traditional psychoanalytic categories of thought to a radically different, relational theory of mind. I introduce my reading by contrasting it with other readings of Fairbairn as a more conventional theorist. I then demonstrate the ways in which Fairbairn's position between paradigms contributed to his difficult struggle with the thorny problem of the motivation for internalization. We will explore the advantages of an alternative approach to internalization that draws on Loewald's notions of boundaryless primary states, or Mode 2. Finally, I illustrate the advantages of Fairbairn's radical innovations by considering two clinical vignettes concerning impulses and guilt, the traditional provinces of classical, pre-Fairbairnian theorizing. By taking a close look at some of the inner tensions in Fairbairn's work, we will get a fuller sense of the scope and multidimensionality of the relational turn in psychoanalysis.

OBJECT-SEEKING: DRIVE OR GROUND?

In Greenberg's (1991) thoughtful and challenging book *Oedipus and Beyond*, he argues that all psychoanalytic theories must contain a theory of drive, either explicitly or implicitly. He then goes on to claim that although Fairbairn presented his object relations theory as an alternative to traditional drive theory, a close reading reveals a hidden drive concept in Fairbairn's vision, a kind of crypto-drive theory. Greenberg believes that unless a theory espouses a complete and thoroughly naive environmentalism (Edgar Levenson is the only proponent he can find of such a viewpoint), a concept of drive is essential. Presuppositions about drive define what the individual brings to interaction with others. Without drives, the individual would be merely passive putty, shaped by external, social influences. In this view, theorists who eschew *Freud's* drive theory necessarily substitute an alternative theory of drive to account for that which draws the individual into interactions with others, and for the way in which the individual records and is shaped by those interactions.

One might ague in response that Fairbairn's object-seeking *is* a kind of drive, in much the same way that Bowlby saw attachment as a drive. Emmanuel Ghent (in press) has suggested naming these kinds of motivations *drives*, with a small d, to distinguish them from *Drives*, with a big D, reserved for Freud's sort of sexual and aggressive drives. But, interestingly, Greenberg argues that Fairbairn's notion of "object-seeking" cannot itself be considered a drive (and I imagine he would feel the same way about "attachment"), because it is too vague and indeterminate. All psychoanalytic theories depict individuals as seeking objects. The question is, What are they seeking objects for? For Freud, objects are sought for sexual and aggressive discharge. For Sullivan, objects are sought for the satisfaction of various integrating tendencies. In itself, as Greenberg reads it, object-seeking means nothing; it is an empty slogan, restating the obvious and making none of the specific motivational claims that make a theory interesting and useful, with all the attendant risks.

So, why *do* babies and other people seek objects? What exactly makes an object an object? An object, Greenberg asserts, can only become meaningful, psychologically speaking, because it serves some purpose, provides some sort of gratification, meets some need. Thus, any object relations theory presupposes some basic need that objects are sought to meet. In Greenberg's reading, Fairbairn believes that objects are sought for the gratification of oral dependency. In this view, Fairbairn has substituted a simplistic one-drive system for the complexity of Freud's dual-drive system. Although Greenberg's analysis is persuasive, and he finds passages in Fairbairn's papers to support it, I believe Fairbairn was also after something more fundamental, which he never developed fully or clearly, and I want to try to get at that radical relational project.

To argue that we need a concept of drive to describe what the individual seeks in interactions with other people presumes that the individual qua individual is the most appropriate unit of study. It assumes that the individual, in his or her natural state, is essentially alone, and then is drawn into interaction for some purpose or need. I believe that Fairbairn, like Sullivan (1953), was struggling toward a different way of understanding the nature of human beings, as fundamentally social, not as *drawn* into interaction, but as *embedded* in an interactive matrix with others as his or her natural state.

In what sense does a bee *seek* other bees? In what sense does the wolf or zebra *seek* other members of his pack or herd? It seems cumbersome and improbable to regard this gregariousness or object-seeking as expressive of a discretely experienced need, like hunger or sex, that emerges from time to time, when the individual bee or wolf or zebra feels lonely, requiring other members of its kind for satisfaction. Many animals are, by their very nature, social beings and can exist as a normal creature of their specific type only as part of the group. Fairbairn, Sullivan, and other architects of the relational model were redefining the nature of the human psyche as fundamentally social and interactive. Fairbairn was suggesting that object-seeking, in its most radical form, is not the vehicle for the satisfaction of a specific need, but is the expression of our very nature, the form through which we become specifically *human* beings.

To define humans as relational is quite different from specifying object-seeking as a specific drive. Human beings are oxygen-breathing organisms; we are not *driven* to seek oxygen (except if it is suddenly withdrawn). It is simply what we are built to do, and we do it without intentionality. Human beings are also language-generating creatures. In the heyday of behaviorism, language was assumed to be an instrumental act that emerged in the individual for some purpose, because it was reinforced. Now language is generally regarded as an emergent property of the human brain. Thus, Pinker (1994) describes language as an instinct precisely because "people know how to talk in more or less the sense that spiders know how to spin webs . . . spiders spin spider webs because they have spider brains, which give them the urge to spin and the competence to succeed" (p. 18). Now there are many controversial theories about the evolutionary adaptive purpose or purposes that originally, eons ago, selected for language development. But, Pinker is suggesting, the young spider does not begin to spin his web because he is hungry or because he intuits his need for webs as the basis of his livelihood, but because spinning webs is what he is designed to do. Similarly, babies do not generate sounds and eventually language for some instrumental purpose, but because they have human brains, and that is what we are wired to do.

Human beings, starting as small babies, seek other human minds to interact with, not for the satisfaction of some discrete need, but because we are wired to respond visually to the human face, olfactorially to human smells, auditorially to the human voice, and semiotically to human signs (Muller, 1996). We are designed, in ways we are just beginning to appreciate, to be drawn into a wide array of reciprocally regulating (Mode 1) interactions and shared (Mode 2) affects with other human beings, and this mutual regulation and sharing is necessary for babies to be able to use their brains to become specifically human, language-generating creatures, with specifically human minds.[1] It was Fairbairn's most far-reaching contribution to be among the first to intuit that the establishment and maintenance of relationships with others is as fundamental to the nature of the human organism as breathing oxygen. Greenberg is right to point to the importance Fairbairn attributes to oral dependency, but, in my view, this reflects not the true, underlying significance of "object-seeking," but rather Fairbairn's incomplete emergence from Freud's own starting point of an individual organism driven by needs.

Greenberg reads Fairbairn as offering a motivational system, necessarily based on drives, rather like Freud's, but lacking the latter's richness and complexity. A closely related but more appreciative reading (Pine, 1990; Eagle, 1993) portrays Fairbairn as offering something new and useful, but something wholly compatible and integratable with classical drive theory and the structural model. Why not combine a one-person *and* a two-person model, the intrapsychic *with* the interpersonal. Winnicott and Khan (1953) wrote an early review of Fairbairn's work in which they criticized him for asking the reader to make a choice between Freud and Fairbairn. But why is a choice necessary? Doesn't it make sense to believe that human beings are *both* pleasure-seeking *and* object-seeking?

This strategy, while admirable in its inclusiveness, reflects a fundamental misunderstanding of what Fairbairn was up to. A "two-person" perspective, the common frame of reference Fairbairn and Sullivan shared, might be defined as follows: The best way to understand persons is not in isolation, but in the context of their relations with others, past and present, internal and external, actual and fantasized. It should be immediately apparent, although this is routinely missed, that such a perspective *includes* individual persons, but sets them in a particular context, which, it is argued, is the preferred context for understanding what is most interesting about them, psychoanalytically speaking.

The argument for a hybrid model that combines one- and two-person perspectives represents a confusion of conceptual levels. It empties out the individual persons from the two-person model and then claims that we need a one-person–two-person hybrid to bring them back. But the individuals were accounted for in the two-person model all along — how could they not be? What would it mean to have a two-person model without individual persons? — a model describing the events between people but not the people themselves? Consider as an analogy the movement in astronomy from an earth-centered model to our current model of the solar system, a shift from a view of the earth in its unique splendor at the center of things to a repositioning of earth in a larger context or field, along with other planets, in orbit around the sun. A hybrid modelist might argue that the earth is not sufficiently represented in the solar model. Why not have both an earth- and a sun-centered model? What we need is a mixed model so we can have it all, or both models in a paradoxical, dialectical tension with each other. But to make that argument, one must first take the earth out of the solar model to justify the need for a hybrid. The solar model provides a full account of the earth, its specific geology, weather systems, flora and fauna, *but in a broader context,* and that is the crucial difference. To explain some things on earth, like the local physics of billiard tables, one need not refer to the sun and other planets. For others, like annual weather cycles, it is crucial. It is never necessary to step out of the solar model; not all parts of it are used in thinking about every problem. A hybrid earth-centered–sun-centered model purchases a shallow inclusiveness at the price of conceptual incoherence.

Similarly, Fairbairn understood very well that human beings seek pleasure. He was not disputing that. What he did suggest was that Freud stopped his account, his understanding of pleasure-seeking, too soon. By making pleasure-seeking a fundamental motivational principle, *the* fundamental motivational principle of drive theory, Freud did not understand it in its proper context, the object-relational field. *Why* do people seek pleasure? For Fairbairn, the best explanation is not that pleasure-seeking, as drive discharge, is a fundamental property of mind, but because pleasure-seeking, like all other dynamic processes, occurs in the context of object-seeking, because pleasure is a powerful medium for the establishment and maintenance of connections with others. This reordering of priorities is precisely what makes Fairbairn's model such a powerful explanatory framework for just the sort of dynamics Freud's hedonic model foundered on: masochism, negative therapeutic reactions, the repetition compulsion. If pleasure-seeking is not available, people seek pain, because pain often provides the most direct, alternative channel to others.

A hybrid model based on the dual principle that people are fundamentally *both* pleasure- *and* object-seeking is certainly a possible framework, but it is no longer Fairbairn's and does not include Fairbairn's, except in a diminished, cardboard-cutout sense. Fairbairn provided an account of pleasure-seeking, recontextualized within object-seeking. The hybrid model takes pleasure-seeking out of Fairbairn's model as a rationale for resuscitating the traditional drive model, just as the astronomical hybrid would have to take earth out of the solar model as a justification for reviving Ptolemaic astronomy. The psychoanalytic hybrid is not a broader perspective, which includes both Freud and Fairbairn, because the Fairbairn it includes is a collapsed version, deprived of its broad, explanatory power. It is a version based on a reading of Fairbairn in which "object-seeking" is understood as a discrete motive propelling an individually constituted organism, like Freud's Drives, rather than as the very nature of that organism, wired to be actualized only through exchanges with other minds.

BOUNDARIES AND PROBLEMS OF INTERNALIZATION

Fairbairn's position between paradigms becomes manifest in his struggle with what he clearly found to be the bedeviling problem of the motivation for early internalization; he kept changing and revising his position on this question from one paper to the next. Because Fairbairn regarded people as most fundamentally reality-oriented, directed toward actual people in the interpersonal world, he wrestled again and again with how and why those actual experiences with real people first get established internally. And the most common criticism (Skolnick, 1998) of Fairbairn's work has been directed precisely at his commitment to the notion that internalization takes place, in the beginning, because early objects are "bad" or "unsatisfying," leaving out the ways in which "good" experiences are taken in.

Fairbairn started off on the wrong foot with regard to this question, because he did not fully appreciate the implications of viewing the individual mind in a relational context with other minds. To pose the question, What is the motive for the first internalization? is to begin with the premise that there is a fundamental differentiation and boundary between inside and outside. This is a premise that Fairbairn inherited from Klein. If something from outside is found inside (which is what we mean by "internalization"), then we have to explain how it got there. Whereas Klein believed that boundary was regularly traversed through fantasy-driven expulsive-projective and incorporative-introjective processes, Fairbairn (1954) thought that internalization was explanable only in terms of specific acts of defense. "I do not regard introjection of the object as the inevitable expression of the infant's instinctive incorporative needs — as something that just happens, so to speak" (p. 16n).

Psychoanalytic authors have been struggling with the central tension between sameness and differentiation at least as far back as Freud's (1921) claim that in the beginning, object cathexis and identification are indistinguishable. If Freud had given what he termed "primary identifications" more weight, he might have moved in the direction that Fairbairn did, depicting libido as object-seeking rather than pleasure-seeking. Fairbairn (1952) picked up the notion of primary identification from Freud to "signify the cathexis of an object which has not yet been differentiated from the cathecting subject" (p. 34). But although Fairbairn mentions primary identifications from time to time, he did not grant them explanatory significance when he came to account for the earliest derivation of our inner worlds. If Fairbairn had given these identifications more weight, he might have regarded primary internalizations as residues of developmentally early object relations, perhaps distinct perceptually, but undifferentiated affectively and psychologically.

What if one assumes there is no discrete psychological boundary for the baby at the start and that the baby begins life fully embedded in a (Mode 1) presymbolic relational matrix composed of interactions with caregivers? What if powerful emotional experiences (Mode 2) transcend the cognitive boundaries between self and others? What if a sense of oneself as a separate individual and of objects as differentiated others is only gradually constructed, over the course of early development, out of this undifferentiated matrix? Then the sense of oneself as populated with presences of early significant objects would not have to be accounted for solely in terms of some discrete, intentional, defensive process. Intensely emotional experiences with others early in life and, on an unconscious level, throughout later life as well, might involve a diffusion of boundaries between self and other, so that it is not possible to know precisely who is who. I am suggesting that such intense emotional experiences, for example, ecstatic sexual intimacy, are being processed on different levels, or in different modes, simultaneously. In Mode 1, there is dense procedural interaction that is deeply felt but not linguistically symbolized at all. In Mode 3, there is a differentiation and a sorting out of who is doing what to whom. In Mode 4, there is a richly personal sense of being recognized by a unique other, whom one recognizes in return. And in Mode 2, there are powerful feelings, intense excitement, and affective sensibilities generated in each partner that are not neatly assignable and become part of each participant's experience of the event. Pleasurable and unpleasurable, good and bad senses of oneself as like one's parents, in fact, *as* one's parents, would be continually rediscovered throughout life, because they would constitute the starting point, the ground out of which a differentiated framework of self and others develops. As we noted in chapter 2, Loewald pointed to the way in which the very concept of the "object," which Fairbairn took for granted, is a developmental construction.

The emphasis Klein and Fairbairn placed on the boundedness of the individual vis-à-vis external objects was an important antidote to the earlier Freudian concept of objectless, primary narcissism. This movement toward a view of the baby as object-related from the start was linked to a view of the baby as separate from the objects he was seeking. This important and useful trend was further developed in the work of some infant researchers (like Stern, 1985), who explored a quite differentiated baby who clearly knows who is who. But this is where viewing mind as organized multiply and variably according to different degrees of differentiation and sophistication is helpful. Perceptual discrimination is very different from affective embeddedness, as current writings on transference-countertransference phenomena make increasingly clear. As Phillips (1995) has put it, "When two people speak to each other, they soon become inextricable: words are contagious" (p. 22).

We need to move toward a more sophisticated way of thinking about the dialectic between union and differentiation, in which they are regarded not as opposites, but as blended together in different forms on different levels (see related concepts in Eigen, 1981; Grotstein, 1990). Thus, it is possible to combine Loewald's notion of a primary affective unity with Stern's notion of perceptual differentiation from objects. We might imagine this tension in terms of the kind of pattern achieved by potters who use crackled glazes, where the surface of the pot is, in one sense, an unbroken unity and, in another sense, is broken into fragments with clear boundaries.

IMPULSES

Theorists and clinicians who value eclecticism in psychoanalytic ideas often point to the utility of drive theory in accounting for the peremptory in human experience, the sense of being "driven" by powerful impulses and by guilt in relation to those impulses. It is compelling to regard impulses as the direct manifestation in the mind of impersonal sexual and aggressive drives, and to regard guilt as an internalized, socially derived reaction to those impulses. Of course, relatedness is important, this eclectic position grants; but body-based impulses are also important. A hybrid model seems the best framework for granting appropriate weight to both these fundamental dimensions.

What is missed in this line of thought is the way in which Fairbairn's radical relationality provided an account, different from classical drive theory, not just of relationships, but of impulses and guilt as well. For Fairbairn, both impulses and guilt *are* relationships. When Loewald's Mode 2 account of shared affect is added to Fairbairn's account of ties to bad objects, an extremely compelling understanding of both impulses and guilt emerges.

George, a man in his mid 20s whose wife had abandoned him as unexciting and distant, discovers in analysis the implications of his early relationship with his uncle, which had been fully sexual, possibly including oral and anal penetration, being dressed in women's clothes, and being tied up. Over several years of productive analytic work these memories and associated dynamics had been extensively explored and, in many respects, relived in the transference with a skilled female analyst. George had allowed himself, with great trepidation, to remember and fantasize about these experiences, which he found degrading and enormously conflictual but also very stimulating. His dormant sexuality began to come alive. Slowly over the course of the analysis he began experimenting with cross-dressing and masturbated to sadomasochistic scenarios provided by similarly oriented individuals on the internet. George had recently begun a relationship with a woman, which he had been finding quite satisfying, emotionally and sexually, but the lure of the memories with the uncle and the various masturbatory forms through which he reenacted them was still powerful. He felt himself to be in the grip of powerful impulses to arouse and satisfy himself through conflictual forms of excitement that had been held in repression for many years.

How are we to understand the nature of these impulses? What are they? Consider a session following a weekend that George had spent with his girlfriend, with whom he had very satisfying sex. As he was saying good-bye to her, George found himself thinking, in a way he regarded as perverse and in contrast to the more wholesome sexual experiences of the weekend, about the always available electronic trysts involving cross-dressing and sadomasochistic playacting. He pushed the thoughts away, wanting instead to savor the weekend, with its sexual and emotional intimacies. But he could not get the thoughts of the electronic possibilities out of his mind. They became more and more exciting and irresistible. He wrestled with them, but unsuccessfully, and on returning home, he found himself succumbing to what he experienced as ego-alien impulses to seek out these kinky masturbatory experiences.

Now, there are many possible ways to understand this sequence. From a hybrid framework, one might regard George as caught in the grips of an intense conflict between the object-seeking of his interpersonal intimacies with the girlfriend and an addictive pleasure-seeking that remained from his early sexual traumas. But that interpretation would not be Fairbairn's, and it would not be making the fullest use of Fairbairn's contributions. Fairbairn wrote about impulses as "disintegration products" of failed personal relations, but the most interesting use to be made of Fairbairn's perspective here is in the unpacking of George's experience of the impulse itself.

As the analyst explored the texture of George's wrestling with his impulses, it began to seem as if that struggle itself repeated his experience with his uncle. The impulse, like the uncle, was a powerful force outside himself, a force that tempted him into something pleasurable but forbidden and frightening, a force that was stronger than he was, a force that eventually overcame him, to which he eventually surrendered. Thus, although he experienced the impulse as a depersonalized tension, a drive perhaps, it seemed clinically most useful to understand it as a pared down, symbolic representation of his uncle. In George's surrender to an overpowering, pleasure-providing impulse, he was reenacting, through an internal object relationship, his object-relational connection to his uncle, which had, in an important sense, become threatened by his more mutual, higher level intimacy with his girlfriend. In Fairbairn's terms, it was the threat to, and allegiance with, his internal relationship with his uncle that was the motive for his actions, not pleasure-seeking in itself.

Fairbairn conceptualized the kind of internal object relation that forms the substructure of impulses like George's in terms of Mode 3 self-object configurations. But the addictive power of sexual impulses like these derives partly from the Mode 2 shared affects that they contain. George's experiences with his uncle provided some of the most intense, passionate moments of his childhood. The excitement, the sense of drama, mystery, the forbidden that characterized his uncle's experience also became George's experience. George's lustful impulses were not just vehicles to tie him *to* his uncle; they also *were* his uncle, and, through the boundary-permeable affective intensity of those moments, they were *George himself,* at his most excited, most adventurous, most alive.

Adhesive attachments to impulses have often been described as "addictive," which captures something of the phenomenology of these experiences. Until recently, "addictive" was a metaphor; George's surrender to his impulses was *like* taking a drug. But recent advances in neurophysiology have made it possible to understand addictive object-relations as true chemical addictions. Van der Kolk (1994) and others have suggested that endorphin pathways are laid down in the brain over the course of the first several years of life, in the context of early object relationships. Affectively intense experiences, both positive and negative, are accompanied by endorphin release, and these chemically bathed states in the brain thus become associated with states of both deep security and trauma. There is thus a physiology of attachment in these ties to early objects. Early experiences are addictive, not just because of their psychological salience but also because of their neurochemical concomitants.

There are many people who feel overcome by their rage, rather than their sexuality. Dan, another patient, remembered the many times his father would blow up in volcanic explosions and beat him. And he himself, as a grown man, felt periodically overcome by similar violent bursts of temper. As we came to understand, Dan experienced his father as thoroughly controlled by his mother in virtually every way imaginable, and he felt a secret thrill in his father's explosions, even though he was also the terrified victim of them. In regarding rage, both in his father and in himself, as a depersonalized force of nature, he was celebrating what Fairbairn would understand as a Mode 3 libidinal tie to his father, outside of the mother's purview. In adding Mode 2 concepts, we could also say that Dan's affective organization centered around the emotional power he shared with his father during the latter's outbursts, even when he himself was the victim of them. And the physiology of those outbursts, the aroused excitement that accompanied them and the cathartic calm that followed them, played an important role in preserving aggressive impulses as a conflictual, split-off domain of Dan's experience.

Fairbairn (1954) speaks of patients who identify their genitals with the exciting object, as something external to their central self that entices and lures them and to which they surrender. These kinds of patients, like George, illustrate the utility of not regarding object relations as on a distinct and equal footing with pleasure-seeking or sexuality and aggression, in a spirit of eclecticism. Among the most radical implications of the perspective that Fairbairn was developing is the notion that the experience of sexuality and aggression does not represent the eruption of sheer biology into subjective experience, but that these experiences are shaped, their meaning determined, their location within the matrix of multiple self-organizations fixed, by early object relations.

Further, in the synthetic relational framework proposed here, George's sense of his uncle and his perverse connections to him as a powerful and reliable internal presence does not have to be accounted for, as Fairbairn believed, as the result of a discrete psychic event of internalization. They might also be regarded as the residues of early experiences in which the uncle and those intense moments with him were experienced as part of George himself, in the context of general parental neglect and an absence of intense emotional experiences that would have been more constructive and affirming.

GUILT

Will, a 45-year-old corporate executive, came for psychoanalysis because "bad" dreams made it very difficult for him to sleep at night. The dreams portray diffuse anxiety situations in which he has a great deal to do and is intensely nervous about having forgotten something, which will mushroom into a disaster. In reality, he has a great deal of responsibility on his job, and sometimes the content of the dreams refers to actual concerns and obligations. He is very dubious about psychoanalysis, but he feels desperate about his sleep problems. His wife is a believer in psychoanalysis, thinks he has deep emotional conflicts, and convinces him to come.

Not too many sessions into our work, Will revealed that he thinks of his life as having suffered a kind of disaster 15 years before from which he has not really recovered. He had been married previously, from his early to his late 20s, to Gail, a woman he thought he loved. He had begun a flirtation with Anne that turned into an affair; and he found himself, despite desperate efforts, simply unable to give it up. The affair began during his wife's pregnancy, and, when his daughter was two years old, he left to live alone for four years. During this time, he did not allow himself to be with Anne, tried several times to return to Gail, felt extremely tortured with having left his wife and daughter and for not having told Gail the truth about the existence of another woman. Finally, he told Gail about Anne, but that only made things worse. Eventually, Anne gave him an ultimatum—marry her or the relationship was over. He married her, and they have been more or less happily married, with two children, for the past ten years.

The problem is that he cannot forgive himself for what he did to Gail and his daughter. Nor will Gail forgive him. In their financial and pragmatic dealings over time with the daughter, he is overly accommodating, to the great distress of Anne. Gail was the only child of close-binding parents who had lovingly, in some sense suffocatingly, taken Will into their family and adopted his large family as their own. They were devastated by the breakup of their daughter's marriage. Will feels he has damaged their lives as well. It did not take long for us to recognize that the dreams might not refer only to his work situations, but also to his sense of failed obligations with respect to his first marriage. He recalled that a horrible aspect of his trysts with Anne was the nagging sense that something terrible might happen to Gail and his daughter while he was off enjoying himself.

Despite his wife's prodding, Will avoided psychotherapy for many years because he was dubious about the whole idea of unconscious motivation. More important, he viewed psychoanalysis as part of a modern (perhaps postmodern) culture that allows people to avoid taking responsibility for their actions. He loathes public officials who do terrible things, betraying the public trust and their private relationships, who then appear on television saying something facile like, "Mistakes were made. I was wrong. But how big of me to admit my crimes; everybody makes mistakes. Please vote for me in the next election." Will is afraid that I will try to explain away his past actions and talk him out of his guilt, which he thinks he *should* maintain, if he is to retain any sense of integrity. Yet, it is incomprehensible to him that he did what he did, and he often found himself in gatherings of friends making long, intense speeches criticizing people for doing precisely what he himself had done.

Will is one of five children of first-generation immigrant parents. His father's father was a very hardworking man whose working-class job disappeared during the depression. Will's father had to give up plans to go to law school in order to support his younger siblings. Will's parents worked extremely hard and saved their money in order to put their own children through college and graduate school, and they succeeded admirably. Will's father died quite a few years ago, but he remains an extremely powerful presence in Will's life, as an ideal figure whose devotion to family was a superordinate value. Part of the pain of Will's own life is the sense that his father, who never met Anne, could never have understood how he could have betrayed his first wife and child.

My first take on Will's story (countertransferencially speaking) was one of admiration. I felt he was right to feel guilty for what he had done, and I admired his social critique of facile, psychopathic posturing by public figures. After a while, I felt he had suffered enough. (Of course, all these reactions were mediated through my own marital history, values, conflicts over guilt, and so forth.) We explored in detail his childhood conflicts and guilt in relation to both parents, his experiences of his two wives, the way in which each wife represented a different aspect of himself and his family history, and so on. Although he viewed his adultery as a sexual fall of almost Biblical proportions, it became clear that his second wife made possible the expression of an entirely different dimension of him, one concerned with fun and pleasure, whereas his first wife fit into the extremely dutiful, often anhedonic themes of his family of origin. (Of course, it was much more complicated; I am being very reductive here for purposes of brevity.) He began to feel now, knowing more about himself as he did (partly through our work), that he should have consulted a couple therapist at the time. I agreed. Perhaps the first marriage could have been saved. He really did not think so, but at least he would have felt later that he had tried. But none of this seemed to ease his self-punitive guilt.

How should we understand Will's guilt? The traditional psychoanalytic assumption would be that this guilt about an act in his adulthood masked an earlier oedipal guilt for forbidden sexual desires. This model suggests that interpreting the underlying childhood, fantasied crime would relieve the suffering. Fairbairn believed that guilt was often the vehicle for a powerful, underlying object tie, and that trying to relieve the guilt would merely drive the attachment to the internal object deeper into repression. Indeed, Will's fierce determination not to let himself off the hook seemed to suggest precisely what Fairbairn predicted.

The (Mode 3) self-object configuration underlying Will's guilt seemed to entail an attachment to the enormously perfectionistic standards of his parents, particularly his father, whom he loved and admired deeply. His badness kept alive their imagined goodness as an internal presence toward which he could aspire; his badness held out the hope that some day he would be good enough to win their love and be at one with them. Adding Mode 2 concerns enriches this picture. Will's father also seemed to suffer considerable guilt in his approach to life, manifesting itself in a guilt-tinged religiosity and a total devotion toward his own mother at the expense of his wife and children. Will accompanied his father both on pilgrimages to his grandmother and to Church; his own guilt seemed to preserve something of the affective intensity of these shared experiences with his father.

Several different interactions between us contributed to deepening the work and transforming Will's experience in ways that I find illuminated by the most radical implications of Fairbairn's perspective.

One turning point followed what might be considered a countertransference enactment, in which I took on the role of the "bad" guilt-inducing object. I had begun to find Will's guilt a bit sanctimonious. He was going on about his concessions to Gail over holiday plans, in which his daughter, as usual, would spend most of the holiday with her mother; he would bend himself out of shape to make this possible, and Anne, as usual, was angry and resentful. What struck me, for the first time, was how little time his daughter had spent with Will's extended family, which consisted of all kinds of interesting aunts, uncles, and cousins. In deferring to Gail, his daughter's life had been truncated around the small family comprised of her mother and grandparents, when in reality she had another bigger family of which she was deprived. When I encouraged Will to explore his feelings around these choices, he conjured up an image of Gail and her parents at the holiday table, with an empty chair, the one his daughter would have to vacate, like that of Tiny Tim at the end of Dickens's *A Christmas Carol*. He had ripped this family apart by leaving, and he was bound to do whatever he could to ease their continuing pain.

Out of an initial irritation, of which I became aware only retrospectively, I asked him what he thought his daughter would feel when she had grown up and tried to understand why she had been deprived of time with his extended family. Was she being deprived to ease his guilt? It struck me for the first time that, rather than actually *bearing* the guilt for what he had done, Will was denying it by appeasing Gail, as if he could, in fact, buy her off for his crime. By fixing this image of the family that was rendered asunder and still missed him (Gail, by the way, had actually remarried), he was fixing it in time, so that his crime could still be atoned for rather than become an actuality of the past. My guilt-provocation and subsequent interpretation had a big impact on him. (Eventually, his concern about my values and appeasing them became a focus for exploration.)

From where in the complex interactive transference-countertransference mix between us did this intervention emerge? In one sense (Mode 3 enactment), I was speaking with the voice of his parents, blaming him for doing something bad. This unwitting repetition of an old self-other configuration enabled me to open up the closed circle of his self-punitive guilt, so that old patterns might be considered and transformed. In another sense (Mode 2 shared affect), my irritability at Will grew out of my own feelings of guilty urgency about the destructive impact that he (and I, through my inability to have an impact on him) was having on his daughter. What becomes analytically useful about transference-countertransference enactments is the possibility of old patterns becoming opened up and transformed. As we processed the guilt induced in him by me in relation to his managing his time with his daughter, he was able to open up and change his behavior in ways that were growth-enhancing for both of them. This contrasted with the destructive guilt he had been torturing himself with in relation to his past, which served only as a self-punishment in the service of an illusory atonement, the kind of static arrangement that Loewald (1978a) referred to as the "corruption of the superego."

Several other interchanges between us seemed to have an important impact on opening up Will's tightly knit mortification. They involved what we might think of as (Mode 4) explorations and recognitions of Will's own unique subjective experience, in contradistinction to the (Mode 3) identifications he had inherited from his parents and had tenaciously maintained.

One line of inquiry began with an exploration of Will's flirtations with other women during the course of his first marriage, events that he treated as unexplainable aberrations. I suggested that he had difficulty in acknowledging to himself various aspects of his own sexuality and sense of adventure that were impossible for him to integrate into his first marriage; these qualities were very important in drawing him toward his second wife and found a satisfying place in his second marriage. In these experiences he was different from his father, in ways he had trouble coming to terms with, and the narrative of his seduction by Anne and his fall from grace served to externalize this facet of himself, thereby making him incomprehensible to himself.

A second line of inquiry involved Will's struggle with religion. He had been raised in the Catholic church, but his church attendance had lapsed when he was in college. Now, although not particularly religious, he was interested in attending church and possibly in providing religious education for his children. His marital status as a divorced and remarried man, however, created obvious problems. He said a return to the church was impossible. I did not know too much about this, but asked a lot of questions, and it turned out that there *were* congregations to which it was likely he would be able to belong. The problem was, he did not approve of those congregations. Eventually, I noted that he seemed to be protecting a particular ideal of the church from corruption by people like himself.

Later we explored his stance on divorce, which I suggested seemed to involve his upholding the church's position on the irreversibility of marriage. He felt misunderstood. As a progressive intellectual, he did not abide by the church's teachings on these things, including his acceptance of birth control and abortion. As we discussed these different issues, it became apparent that although he valued the church's teachings on issues like the sacredness of prenatal life, he felt there was a broader context — third-world poverty, for example — that required a reconsideration of those ideals in the light of other concerns. I suggested that he had not been similarly able to recontextualize and up-date the ideal of marriage taken from his parents. The fact that his second marriage was so much more satisfying seemed to have no bearing on his holding onto the ideal of the indissolubility of his first marriage. We agreed that there was something at stake in preserving a sense of continuity with his father and his ideals, despite the price it exacted from him in terms of guilt.

Over the course of several months, during the second year of treatment, things began to change. Will drew clearer lines in his negotiations with Gail and began to appreciate ways in which his guilt was punishing toward Anne. He gradually found himself committing himself to his second marriage, owning it in ways he had previously been unable. He recently had the following dream.

> Anne and I were walking to the train station, as if going to work. There was a crowd of people. We missed the train, and then tried to take an elaborate walk around the perimeter of the station to get to another entrance to catch the next train. We were going down a covered walkway into a tunnel. To get to the train platform, you had to go up a ladder. Anne went ahead of me. Ahead of her another guy climbed up into a square opening of light and stepped out of sight. As soon as Anne disappeared in that opening, a train suddenly rushed by. I realized with horror that the opening was onto the tracks themselves. The train must have hit her. Car after car went by; it seemed as if it were taking forever. After the last car, I sprang up to look around. On a patch of grass, Anne and several other people were sitting. They were all alive, shaken, with bumps and bruises, but no serious injuries. Anne was crying and I went to comfort her. I looked up, and standing there was my mother and my (deceased) father. They looked like they did in the 1970s, before they got very gray. It was a miracle. Anne could see them too. Then they comforted Anne also, and we all embraced.

Despite his doubts about psychoanalysis and dream interpretation, Will saw this dream as highly significant, representing his own acceptance of Anne in a way he hadn't before, and a reconciliation of the part of him that was involved with her with the part of him that was devoted to his parents' ideals. The only thing I added was that I thought it might be interesting to think of the train, with the slow violence of car after passing car, as him as well, in his relentless violence toward Anne and the part of himself that was connected with and had come alive in his relationship with Anne. He resonated strongly with this notion.

For me, this example illustrates the power of using Fairbairn's model in its most radical form, rather than collapsing it to create hybrids. Will was involved with pleasure-seeking and guilty impulses, to be sure. But the more useful framework for understanding his struggles comprehended pleasure-seeking and guilt in the context of conflictual allegiances to significant others, present and past, internal and external, actual and fantastic. Interestingly, such a framework makes it possible to regard guilt with greater existential vividness and centrality than the customary psychoanalytic reduction to infantile themes. Guilt can be understood as reflective of the very real and inevitable betrayals generated by conflicting loyalties to multiple significant others and multiple versions of oneself.

Will's dream also raises the question of the fate of good objects, good experiences with objects, and, ultimately, the fate of the analytic object. Because Fairbairn regarded internal objects as compensatory substitutes for crucial missing connections with actual others, relative progress and health is depicted as a kind of exorcism. This seems right to me, but not sufficient. I believe good and loving experiences, like bad and hateful experiences, also leave internal residues, sometimes not wholly integratable with each other because they contain intensely affective (Mode 2) experiences organized into (Mode 3) different, multiple versions of self with others. We make the fullest use of Fairbairn's contribution when we explore the ways in which residues from the past can coexist, interpenetrate and enrich experience in the present, much in the way Fairbairn's thinking of a half century ego enriches our experience today.

CHAPTER 6

INTERSUBJECTIVITY
Between Expressiveness and Restraint In
The Analytic Relationship

We live in a psychoanalytic age in which many of the basic underpinnings of the classical model of mind and theory of the analytic situation have become untenable. There are many reasons for this in terms of developments both within and outside of psychoanalysis proper (see Racker, 1968; Levenson, 1972, 1983; Greenberg, 1991; Maroda, 1991, 1999; Mitchell, 1993, 1997; Davies and Frawley, 1994; Gill, 1994; Aron, 1996; Renik, 1996; Benjamin, 1998; Bromberg, 1998; Hoffman, 1998). The central, enormously impactful shift has been the realization that the analytic relationship is no longer usefully understood as the sterile operating theater Freud believed it could be.[1] The analytic relationship is not as different from other human relationships as Freud wanted it to be. In fact, the intersubjective engagement between patient and analyst has become increasingly understood as the very fulcrum of and vehicle for the deep characterological change psychoanalysis facilitates. This has made it impossible to sustain the pragmatic dissociations that aided earlier generations of analysts in their management of the often intense feelings that are generated on both sides of the analytic relationship.

Consequently, there has been considerable focus in recent years on many dimensions of relationality in the interaction between analysand and analyst. As the analyst's inevitable participation in the process has been increasingly investigated, there has been considerable interest in the analyst's passionate feelings about the patient. I would like to explore this topic both because of its central clinical importance and also because it illustrates the ways in which various modes of relationality converge in the dense interactions of transference-countertransference.

One of the most impactful features of the postclassical literature is that it has sometimes been dramatically emancipatory in tone. This was in contrast to the manner in which classical theory of technique, in its antiseptic practices, was largely prohibitive. The student-analyst in classical times (Gill, 1994) was best served by an attitude of general, pervasive restraint. Neutrality, anonymity, and abstinence are all essentially negative principles—they describe what *not* to do. When in doubt, don't answer, don't talk, don't express, don't disclose. Silence and emotional flatness are safe. One of the most dramatic features of the postclassical literature of the past couple of decades has been a sense of liberation. "Look what I did and how useful it was": self-disclosure, a wide assortment of breaks in the so-called frame, and a deep emotional engagement with the patient.

These developments, from my point of view, have been all to the good, opening up very important and useful options for analytic clinicians and, equally important, making it possible for clinicians to be more honest with others and with themselves about what has really been going on. If the literature informed by classical theory of technique was dominated by a tone of restraint, the literature informed by postclassical theory of technique has added, alternating with restraint, an emancipatory tone of expressiveness. The analyst is not a blank screen; the analyst's feelings, including passionate feelings, are inevitably part of the process and, often, usefully so.

Most advances in the history of ideas emerge as reactions to the problems of earlier ideas. One problem in some of the postclassical clinical literature has been that in the emancipatory, expressionist zeal, concerns with restraint have been associated with the older classical prohibitions. Self-revelation, both to the patient and to one's readers, sometimes seems to have become an end and a virtue in itself. All analytic writing necessarily lends itself to misreading in one direction or another; thus, often the first reaction to innovative relational papers that include the disclosure of personal material sometimes is "That was very brave of you." For some readers, there seems to be an implicit assumption that the more said, the better, and that the only reason for restraint, both with one's patients and with one's readers, is a cowardly hiding behind anachronistic classical principles, as if the blank screen has become a hiding place for the fainthearted.[2]

This feature of the way in which the postclassical literature has sometimes been understood has made it easy for the more conservative critics to raise the alarm that, with the abandonment of classical principles, "anything goes." Relationally oriented clinicians are not infrequently portrayed as wild analysts, doing and saying anything that occurs to them in an unrestrained fashion. This criticism is understandable, but ill-founded. In my experience, relational clinicians tend to be a quite thoughtful, careful lot, who operate with a great deal of restraint. And a careful reading of the relational literature suggests a considerable emphasis upon disciplined self-reflection, or what Hoffman (1998) calls "ritual," as a background for spontaneity.[3] There is a small sect, one variety of classical interpersonal analyst, whom I think of as the "it's-all-grist-for-the-mill" or "blurt-it-out school." They sometimes seem to think that "authenticity" requires them to say whatever is on their minds. The fact that Ferenczi, who was so important in the move toward greater authenticity on the part of the analyst, also dabbled in "mutual analysis" with an episodically free-associating analyst has contributed to the confusion. But for the vast majority, in our actual practice, clinical work is quite disciplined, saturated with considerations of caution.

At times it has seemed as if discussions of restraint in the literature were impeded by an aura of political incorrectness. Recent investigations of the presence of the "third" in the analytic situation as a shaping, constraining force represent constructive efforts to grapple with this problem. Lacanians speak of the symbolic register and the Law of the Father; Altman (1996) has referred to the larger cultural context as a third element; and Greenberg (1999) has described the limiting presence of the analytic community. One of the major obstacles to thinking and writing about contemporary relational technique in general is that we have yet to work out a way of fully taking into consideration both expressiveness and restraint in theorizing about clinical technique. This problem becomes particularly acute when we begin to think about the place of feelings of love and hate in the analytic relationship.

AFFECT AND INTENTIONALITY*

A first pass at the topic, according to current relational principles, might suggest a pretty simple, straightforward approach. Whereas love and hate were theorized *out* of the analytic relationship in the classical model, they are theorized back into the analytic relationship in relational theory. Because the analytic relationship is regarded as two-person, interactive, and mutual, love and hate appear in the analytic relationship in much the same fashion as they appear in other intimate relationships. The patient's love and hate, although drawing on past relationships and infantile passions, are also real reactions to real interpersonal exchanges with the analyst, and the latter need to be taken into account. The analyst's love and hate are inevitable, because patients are alternatively doing things that are unavoidably lovable and hateful, and also because the analyst, no matter how mature or well positioned in terms of his own personal life, inevitably and necessarily becomes deeply emotionally involved in the work with his patients. Maroda (1991, 1999) has insightfully explored this perspective on the "two-person" relationship of analyst and patient, and regards "surrender" of the analyst to a deep emotional engagement with the patient as a precondition to effective treatment. It might seem as if the only problem regarding love and hate in the analytic relationship ought to concern the analyst's judgment about the clinical implications in specific circumstances of concealing or expressing his love or hate. (Maroda provides some helpful guidelines with regard to the analyst's self-disclosure.)

But things are actually more complex. The ways in which love and hate emerge in the analytic relationship are *not* simply like the emergence of love and hate in other intimate relationships. Our problem seems simple and straightforward only if we assume love and hate themselves are simple and straightforward.

Love and hate seem like the most natural things in the world. Sometimes they take us completely by surprise, as in the involuntary sigh, accompanying desire, that might escape us at the sight of a beautiful, sexy person, or in a strong, sudden antipathy we might feel in encountering something or someone perceived as hideous or

---

*I am using this term not in the technical, philosophical sense of "aboutness" but to convey the sense of purposiveness, conscious and unconscious.

repellent. Sometimes love and hate feel natural because they occur in relationships we already recognize and understand as loving or hateful, as in an intense flutter of desire or fondness for a longstanding lover or an intense shudder of hatred toward a longstanding enemy. These kinds of experiences contribute to creating the impression that feelings just emerge, unwilled and unbidden, unconstructed. They seem to just happen. But love and hate in long-term relationships, like the analytic relationship, do not just happen. They are shaped and cultivated within contexts that are constructed slowly, over time.

I worked with a man a number of years ago whom I came to think of as the most cultivated person I'd ever met. He was brilliant, born to a very wealthy, sophisticated family, extremely well traveled, and educated at the best schools. He came for treatment because he had trouble imagining what he could possibly live for once his children, whom he loved, had grown and moved away. He began to describe the desolation of his marriage, and he told me about other women he had been involved with before his relationship with his wife. I knew one of these women slightly. He was trying, very unsuccessfully, to remember why he had broken off their relationship. I had found her to be a quite engaging, witty, beautiful, vibrant, sexy women, and was interested to know why he had stopped seeing her. He said it had something to do with her coloring and style — that it did not correspond to the idea he had developed of what a beautiful woman was. I asked him how he felt when he was with her. After a pause of several moments, he said that he had never really thought about it in that way, but that he thinks he actually found her exciting to be with. Now, we could understand this in terms of repressed impulses, but I don't think that does it justice. Through this and similar examples, we came to understand his experience in terms of highly cultivated tastes, which were often at some remove from his actual, visceral sensations. He had ideas, often very rich and textured ideas, about beauty in the arts, music, literature, food, and women. Those ideas opened up certain kinds of experiences and closed off others. When they worked, as in his appreciation of sculpture, his cultivated ideals made possible visceral, sensual experiences of great depth and passion. When his aesthetic commitments overrode his visceral reactions, as had happened with women, his experience had become barren.

We all construct contexts and cultivate relationships in which certain kinds of loves and hates can develop and others are foreclosed.

One of the most challenging and difficult aspects of Schafer's (1976) "action language" metatheory was his argument that emotions are actions. This does not imply voluntarism, or mean that we can decide at a moment's notice what to feel about someone, but that what we feel is generated in the context of what philosophers have termed "intentionality," what we *want* to feel, consciously and especially unconsciously. Thus, Schafer argues that emotions are actions that "define, as they are defined by, the agent's situations; and the agent defines, as he or she is defined by, these situations, actions, and modes" (p. 356). Or, in Farber's (1976, 1999) terms, our loves and hatreds always include a dimension, not of willfulness — conscious, stubborn determination — but of the will, the ongoing agentic shaping of our lives.

It is easy to miss the dimension of intentionality in feelings like love and hate, because love and hate can feel so pure and spontaneous, as if they are the simple, primitive building blocks of experience. They are not. By calling emotions "actions," Schafer was pointing to their underlying complexity, their agentic structure. Loving or hating somebody, in contrast to fleeting arousal, admiration, repugnance, or disapproval, takes time and psychic work. We don't love or hate somebody unless we want to, unless we feel we have good reasons, consciously and, especially, unconsciously. The development of love and hate takes cultivation, nurturing, willful intent. Keeping romantic love alive, and close friendships, requires effort; you have to *want* to do it, consciously and unconsciously, despite the considerable risks. Keeping hate alive, enemies worth despising, requires effort; you have to *want* to do it. Thus, love and hate are not simply spontaneous happenings; they serve complex purposes.

Over the past decade or so, several of us have tried to find ways of capturing the tension in the analytic relationship between the deep involvement of both participants and the differences in the *way* they are involved. Thus, Burke (1992) and Aron (1996) have contrasted the "mutuality" of the analytic relationship with the "asymmetry" of the roles of analysand and analyst. And Ogden (1989) has described the analytic situation as one of "intimacy in the context of formality" (p. 175).

One of the most important distinctions between the role of the analysand and the role of the analyst pertains to the claims on each to be responsible, and this makes their experiences of love and hate quite different. (In chapter 2, we noted Loewald's exploration of these differences.) It is the analysand's job, in some very important ways, to be irresponsible. That is, we ask analysands to surrender to their experience, to show up and discover what they find themselves feeling and thinking. We ask analysands to renounce all other conscious intents. As we all know, this is not easy to do. (It entails a great responsibility of a different sort.) Analysands start out trying to accomplish all sorts of other goals: getting "better" quickly, avoiding trouble, taking care of the analyst, and so on. So, we work with them on articulating their conscious intentions and discovering what would make it safe enough not to pursue them. We are trying to create a context in which the absence of conscious intentions will allow feelings to emerge, feelings like love and hate. These transferential feelings, as I have been suggesting, do not lack intentionality, but their intentions, the most analytically interesting intentions, tend to be unconscious. So we are trying to help make it possible for analysands to surrender themselves to their passions, outside and within the analytic relationship, partially so that they may learn more about those unconscious intentions. We are trying to cultivate in the analysand a kind of analytically constructive irresponsibility.[4]

The analyst's job is similar in some respects and quite different in others. In contemporary analytic thought, in contrast to earlier theory of technique, we also regard the *analyst's* feelings, both outside and within the analytic relationship, as very important. It is important for the analyst to be aware of and to cultivate his feelings, associations, and reveries. But a crucial part of what keeps the analytic situation analytic, what distinguishes the analytic relationship from all other relationships, is precisely that one of the participants, the analyst, is responsible for *keeping* it analytic, always, at all moments.

We could spend a long time discussing exactly what that might mean and how analysts can best do that. I am sure there would be some areas of agreement and some areas of disagreement. But for our purposes here, the most important point is that the analyst is always *trying* to be responsibly analytic, trying to do the "right thing." And what that means is the right "analytic" thing, or the "right thing" as the analyst.

Love and hate in the analytic relationship are quite different, in important respects, for analysand and analyst. We ask of the analysand that he loves and hates irresponsibly, allowing feelings to emerge without conscious screening and concern for their implications and utility. We ask of the analyst that he loves and hates responsibly, allowing feelings to emerge, but never without also taking into account their implications for the analytic process, of which he is the guardian. In this sense, I believe that the kind of "surrender" to emotional engagement Maroda (1999) writes about is always different for the analyst than it is for the analysand. It is because love and hate, despite appearances, are complex states, and the differences between love and hate on either side of the analytic relationship are subtle.

More traditional authors often still tend to regard love and hate as incompatible with the analyst's role, as, in effect, too personal. Schafer (1983), for example, has argued that the analyst's function entails a kind of discipline that requires the "subordination of the analyst's personality" (p. 6). Love and hate, in more passionate forms, would not appear in the countertransference, because they are incompatible with the state of mind Schafer terms the "analytic attitude." I don't experience it that way. I too regard analytic work as entailing a kind of discipline, but I do not feel that my personality is any less present in disciplined analytic work than it is in other activities. Both playing tennis and playing the piano require considerable discipline, but in doing both, I experience my self or personality as being quite involved, although each activity elicits a somewhat different and distinct version of me. The versions of me that emerge in playing tennis, playing the piano, and doing psychoanalysis feel deeply personal, and offer possibilities for experiencing and expressing intense, passionate feelings.

Playing tennis makes possible certain kinds of emotions and sensations: particular forms of sensuality and kinesthetic pleasure, and, depending on the nature of the game, either collaborative intimacy or competitive zeal. Playing the piano makes possible other kinds of emotions and sensations: distinct forms of sensuality, sensory experiences, and conceptual and kinesthetic pleasures, affects evoked by the particular piece, a sense of connection with the composer, and so on. The discipline involved in these activities does not foreclose deep feelings, it facilitates them; but the feelings that emerge are very much shaped by the context. I don't have to keep self-consciously reminding myself that I am playing tennis or playing the piano, but that preconscious intention is always, necessarily, present. For me, the same is true of passion on the analyst's side of the analytic relationship.

Love and hate in the analytic relationship are very complex phenomena. It is not helpful to oversimplify their nature by equating them with love and hate as they appear in other intimate relationships. In my experience, both in my own work and in the supervision of others, love and hate emerge on both sides of the intersubjective engagement of the analytic relationship, but they have their own distinct qualities, different from love and hate in other contexts, and different for the two participants in the analytic relationship.

The analysand is asked to love and hate with abandon, an abandon that would be extremely reckless in any other context. "Love and hate without knowing in advance where these passions will take you," we say to them, mostly implicitly. "Let yourself experience all these feelings that you have always regarded as most dangerous, so we can understand them, sort them out, and make them less terrifying." What makes it possible for the analysand to feel safe enough to love and hate with abandon? In earlier decades, we might have thought it was the analyst's neutrality, anonymity, and abstinence that inspired such confidence. But there is now a widespread appreciation of how dangerous it is to love and hate with abandon an other who is hiding and posturing noninvolvement. What makes it possible to love and hate with abandon is involvement with an other who has feelings in return, sometimes even love and hate, but who is working to employ the feelings on both sides of the relationship in the service of analytic work — constructive, insightful growth and development.

In these days of radically broadened options for clinical work, the one shibboleth always evoked to define the boundary of what one *cannot* do is have sex with the patient. Renik (1996) and Gabbard (1996) have argued that the reason for this is that it violates accepted cultural norms of professional standards. I think this is true, but there is more to it than that. Having sex and either playing tennis or playing the piano are physically incompatible, at least in my experience so far. Having sex and practicing psychoanalysis are emotionally incompatible. The key problem is responsibility. The sensations of sex are too intense not to get lost in them, at the expense of reflecting on analytic implications. Anybody capable of actually doing that would be too creepy to be a good analyst anyway.

This extreme hypothetical helps us think about passion in the analytic relationship. Love and hate are inevitable, both in the transference and in the countertransference. But in the latter, love and hate are only constructive when they emerge in the context of analytic responsibility. Of course, analytic work is full of surprises, and the analyst is likely to find himself occasionally with feelings that are both unexpected and potentially disruptive. But neither falling in love with nor drifting into a chronic hatred toward a patient is compatible with ongoing analytic work; both necessitate consultation and the consideration of possible termination of the treatment. Analytic responsibility is thus a shaping, limiting factor in the intentionality that constructs passion in the analyst. And analytic responsibility in the analyst is a shaping, limiting factor in the intentionality that constructs passion in the analysand. Therefore, the structure of the analytic situation makes possible certain kinds of love and hate and forecloses others. Rather than talking about love and hate in the analytic relationship, we might be more precise to talk about specifically analytic forms of love and hate. I would like to explore some of those forms through a discussion of several brief clinical vignettes.

CARING AND EMPATHY

As we become more deeply involved with a person, as we become fond of him and identify increasingly with him, we *care* more and more about what happens to that person, we take pleasure in his successes and suffer pain at his defeats. The same processes takes place with patients; "caring," a banal word for a complex affective involvement, is centrally important. I don't find myself caring, in the same way, for all my patients; some move me more than others. I think that the way I care or don't care for each one is probably a unique product of the interpersonal chemistry between us. In this sense, the kind of caring I am talking about is related to, but also quite different from, "empathy," at least the way Kohut talked about empathy most of the time.

Empathy, for Kohut, was a methodology, a way of thinking that employs feelings that make possible what he termed "vicarious introspection," imagining what a situation feels like for someone else. The term "empathy" is often used to refer to caring, but I think it is important to distinguish sharply between the two. The sort of caring I am talking about is not a methodology; I don't think it is something that is available early on in an analytic relationship, at least not for me. I just don't care about somebody I've just met in the same way I care about some of the people I've worked with, hard and deeply, for years. The (Mode 2) sharing of affect becomes richer and more subtle over time, and that often generates increasingly deeper caring about the fate of the other.

I had worked with Fred, a child of Holocaust survivors, for about a year and a half. I had found him a very appealing and interesting person from the start. We had worked on a number of different issues and different dimensions of his experience; his intense longing for deeper contact with his father was a central recurring theme. His father was a very tough, explosive man, who had suffered unimaginable losses during the war. There was a sense of warmth, vulnerability, and availability for emotional contact that would manifest itself on very rare occasions, and Fred treasured those memories. But most of the time the father was critical, distant, and paranoid. Fred longed for an emotional and physical intimacy with him, and sometimes tried to provoke moments of contact, but these almost never turned out well. These dynamics manifested themselves in the transference in Fred's great interest in, but extreme caution about, me and my feelings toward him. He noticed that at the beginning of the first session of each week he would feel quite removed and uninvolved, which we were able to trace to a continually recurring sense of my possible disinterest in him, even my resentment toward him.

We had been working on some very important material for several months, which began with a focus on his difficulty falling asleep. He would read well into the night, until sleep sort of overtook him. As we explored this, he realized that he was avoiding the experience of just being alone with himself, without cramming the time with filler until he was overcome by exhaustion. We tentatively began to explore his fantasies about what just being alone with his own mind might be like, and he entered into states of extreme desolation and loneliness connected with his parents' war horrors, which he'd been avoiding his whole life. Part of the experience of speaking with me about these states was my presence there with him, which was very important to him. My experience during these sessions was one of great sadness and desolation (Mode 2), a sense of closeness to and comaradarie with him (Mode 3), and a feeling of privilege that he was allowing me to share these experiences with him (Mode 4). The sense of desolation spread from the content of the sessions to his life in general. At some point, from our mutual feeling that we were working on something very important and useful, there was a transition to his sense that he was now feeling very "remote" from everything, including me and the analysis. He began to report an experience of retreat from the process we had been involved in together.

Over a number of sessions we explored different facets of what had been taking place, and I offered the possibility that he was finding it difficult to bear having let me matter enough to him, to be important enough to accompany him into those desolate psychic landscapes. Tears accompanied his recognition of the accuracy of that statement. We were both silent for quite a while; I found the moment very moving, and wanted to say something, although I really had no idea what to say. Eventually I said something like, "I can see how difficult it is for you to allow yourself to let me be this important to you. I wish there were some way for it to be not so painful, but I can't imagine how that could be." In subsequent sessions, Fred returned to comment on how important that moment was to him. He said it felt as if I had done something with him that his father had never done; it felt as if I were putting my arm around him, being with him, and that mattered a great deal.

I find it useful, retrospectively, to separate my participation in that interaction into two parts: the first statement, or interpretation, which involved a tentative understanding I had about what he was going through, and the second remark, which was an expression of what I *felt about* what he was going through. That remark was a report of my experience. There are many occasions on which I would not report such experience; part of the discipline of analytic work is often precisely keeping quiet about one's concern for a patient's pain. For many patients at various points, they have enough problems without having to be concerned about where you are. (Slochower, 1996, has extensively explored situations in which intersubjectivity, in the sense of explicit articulation of the analyst's reactions, is usefully kept in the background.) In this situation, in which the question of his isolation and the nature of the emotional connection between us was so much in the foreground, it seemed analytically crucial to do.

LOVE AND THE EROTIC

There are some situations when the analyst's love for the patient becomes more intense and erotically tinged. Yet, there are important differences between fleeting feelings of arousal or longing and a passion that can only flourish if cultivated. There are times when a tolerance for sustaining a certain level of arousal seems analytically useful. What is crucial to me is the analyst's struggle to sort out, as best he can, whatever pleasure he might be taking in the situation from the patient's best analytic interests.

In my work with Gloria, the erotic dimension seemed central over the course of several years. She had had, in effect, two fathers: her actual father, a very detached man, who had been away in military service during long stretches of her early years, and an uncle, her mother's brother, in whose house she and her mother had lived during some of the father's absences. Gloria had a deep, passionate relationship with the uncle, which remained in the shadows. Once the father returned, the uncle withdrew as a steady presence; the father never seems to have been able to establish his own relationship to his daughter. Gloria's romantic life was, not surprisingly, split between the man she was supposed to be having a relationship with and shadowy fantasized lovers. In one sense, she sought out psychoanalysis precisely to establish and explore such a romantic love in safe terms that would not threaten her marriage.

Our analytic relationship was characterized by a romantic tension and subtle erotic flirtation on both our parts. I did not self-consciously choose to be flirtatious, but I also did not self-consciously restrain ways of being with her that might be construed as potentially flirtatious. I worried that the pleasure I took in our relationship might cloud my judgment about the ways in which I thought it was being helpful to her. It was clear that my ideas about our usefully bringing to life her buried relationship with her uncle contributed to cultivating (through Mode 1 interactions and Mode 2 shared affect) an emotional context between us that made flirtation possible. She would comment on this quality between us from time to time; my declining to challenge her clearly was understood by both of us to be a corroboration that I sometimes experienced our relationship that way as well. During this period of time, lasting several years, she grew in ways we both regarded as very constructive. The romance between us had very much the quality of a kind of Winnicottian "potential" space; it came alive in the sessions and was carried with her between sessions as a constructive intrapsychic presence. It seemed to live in a world made possible by our acknowledging its presence, as with my work with Becky (chapter 3), but not speaking about it too directly or examining it too closely. We came to understand it as, partially, a re-creation of her romance with her uncle, which was, of course, doomed, hostage to the finality represented by the real father's return.

At some point, several years into the work, things started to feel differently to me. Gloria's fantasies began to feel obsessive; her life, rather than continuing to open, seemed to be collapsing around the analysis. I can't remember what she said exactly, but at some point it became clear to me that she believed that a love affair between us was quite possible, after, if not during, our analytic work together, so I raised the question of her beliefs about this in quite clear, literal terms. At some point in these discussions I told her I would never have an affair with a patient, during or after treatment. My pointing to a limit in what was possible between the two of us evoked both her father's rejection and her uncle's withdrawal. This ushered in a difficult, painful, but also very important period in our work. She became much more engaged than ever before with her husband and other important men in her life. The gains she made became consolidated, and her relationships with other men deepened.

The potential spaces psychoanalysis makes possible — sometimes potential spaces filled with romantic love — have a life span. They can be enormously analytically useful, but only for a while. Then they become constricting. There is a great delicacy in finding a constructive balance between cultivated and questioned love in the transference and the countertransference. Who makes these decisions? Of course, they are made to some extent collaboratively. But I think it is disingenuous to assign the patient equal responsibility for these judgments regarding timing. Ultimately it falls to the analyst to make decisions about the constructive versus destructive implications of various affects in both participants in the analytic process, even though there is no way to make those judgments purely objectively.[5] Part of the analyst's responsibility is to participate in and enjoy that love, while it seems facilitative of the analytic process, but not to enjoy that love so much that it becomes a vehicle for the analyst's own pleasure in a way that occludes his focus on the patient's well-being.

EXASPERATION AND HATRED

Similar considerations apply to exasperation and hatred in the transference and countertransference. Aggression can be an important source of growth for certain patients at certain times during the analytic process, and the kind of aggression that is often useful is an irresponsible hate, a hate without regard for the impact on the other, the kind of all-out hatred that is sometimes associated with Winnicott's (1971) phrase "the use of the object." But some forms of hate are self-destructive as well as other-destructive, undercutting the possibility of the analysand getting any help from analytic work, the kind of spoiling hatred that Klein (1975) depicts in her writing on envy. An all-out hatred or chronic, intractable resentment in the analyst toward the patient is incompatible with a constructive analytic process. Yet, episodic, even hateful exasperation is in some treatments a crucial and perhaps inevitable avenue into the patient's deepest struggles. It is part of the analyst's job to make continual judgments as to the nature of the patient's hatred and the nature of his own, and determine, as best he can, whether it is enhancing or impeding the analytic process.

I have had experiences where it seemed as if the transformations of hate and exasperation in the transference and the countertransference were a major scene of the action in the process for long stretches of time.

Helen, a successful corporate executive, came from a family in which there was enormous, malevolent hatred. In both the past and the present, she experienced her father as demanding, intrusive, and crushing and her mother as cool, detached, and self-absorbed. Primal-scene fantasies, both consciously and as a recurrent motif in her dreams, were of a bloody, sadomasochistic orgy, and the father often hatefully savaged the children, both physically and psychologically, in his desperate exasperation at being unable to reach his wife. She, in turn, was chronically abandoning, unable to protect the children from their father's sadistic voraciousness.

Many of Helen's previous important relationships (including a marriage) had ended in explosive rages, either in her or toward her. And there were chronic, episodic battles between her and me. There would be stretches of time when important work seemed to be getting done, with the content largely focused outside the transference, with enormously intense feelings expressed, often involving great anguish and despair. Then there would be sudden bursts of rage. Helen would abruptly feel that whatever had been taking place, whatever goodness or calm or contact seemed to have transpired, was false for her and coerced by me. She would disclaim, with a profound hopelessness, any value to her of our work, and taunt and mock me regarding any possibility of being helpful to her. I would, in turn, feel quite abused, as she screamed and left, slamming the door so that the whole building shook.

I often felt a deep empathy for Helen during these episodes, because it seemed to me that she was bravely fighting for her psychic survival in an interpersonal context she found crushing. Nevertheless, I was often also the target of her rages, and the combination of her intellectual brilliance and well-earned desperation made her intensely personal attacks sometimes troubling.

I tried many different kinds of responses; often she seemed to find anything I said intrusive and coercive. There were times when I couldn't think of anything else to do, other than simply bear it. During some of those silences I was smoldering, so angry I was unable to think. During some of them I felt a helpless despair. Sometimes I set limits, when I felt her destructiveness toward the work and toward me were reaching points when I felt they threatened our continuing to work together. There were times when I set those limits in an obviously angry and retaliatory tone. Helen took my limit-setting as further expressions of my tyranny, but then would sometimes settle down, chastened, to another period of seemingly constructive work. She was convinced the only reason I continued to work with her was out of a kind of masochistic devotion to duty. I couldn't possibly care about her. This was not true. Although there were certainly times when I felt exasperated and episodically hateful toward Helen, I also often enjoyed and deeply admired her. I liked and cared about her a great deal. But at times when I expressed my enjoyment of her in one way or another, she seemed to find that overstimulating and terrifying.

With the distance that hindsight provides, we could think about the emergence and regulation of rage between us as operating at different interactional levels, consciously and often quite unconsciously: in a Mode 1 "hostile integration" (Sullivan, 1953), in which we struggled for control over both the process and content of the sessions; in a Mode 2 sharing of an affective atmosphere of endangerment and rage; in Mode 3 enactments of various intrapsychic scenarios involving abusers and victims, with Helen and I playing shifting roles; and in Mode 4 struggles over personal recognition and negation, her struggle relating to a desperate need to keep herself psychically alive at any cost, mine growing out of an effort to reach and engage her.

I really don't understand exactly how, but it occurred to me at some point that the quality of our fights was getting better. Were we becoming self-reflective together? She kept trying, and there was something about her efforts that was very moving to me. I found myself able to think better, despite my anger. She stopped storming out; we were getting better at weathering the storms together. One fight was particularly memorable.

At a local bookstore, Helen came across a book I had written. At the next session she lambasted me with a two-pronged attack. The way I presented my work in public sounded as if I were genuine and personal in my work with patients, whereas in reality with her I was formal and schizoid. That was one prong. And then there were times when I interacted with her in a terrifyingly informal way, letting her know how I felt; I didn't seem to grasp her need for a highly professional sort of holding environment. That was the other prong. I was both a hypocrite, acting formally and pretending to be warm, and a dangerous loose cannon, acting warm and unable to maintain a necessary formality. I tried in different ways to describe her conflicts concerning how she wanted me to be, but that just made her angrier. After about a half hour of these attacks, she turned up the heat. "How come I can't get a human response out of you?" she taunted. "I know you are hating me. Why don't you just come out and say it. Look, if we were out on the street, if this weren't an analytic relationship, what would you say to me right now?"

I felt trapped. Given the increasing anger I was feeling, it seemed that either silence or an interpretation would be provocative, yet I couldn't think of anything to say that wouldn't be simply retaliatory. I ended up saying something like, "If this were *not* an analytic relationship, if this were out on the street and you were talking to me this way and I weren't your analyst, I probably would say 'FUCK YOU!' But I *am* your analyst."

She laughed, and I laughed, and the tension was broken. This fight was an important benchmark in the transformation of our relationship into a sustained connection that was much less explosive and deepened over time. She had somehow managed to risk confronting me fully with her hatred while, at the same time, suggesting a kind of transitional space, in the imagined confrontation in the street, in which we might play it out. I had somehow managed to find a way to express my rage and, at the same time, to signal to her that I was not unmindful of my responsibility to take care of her and the process, of which I was the guardian.

Among the important sequelae of this struggle between us around hate was the emergence of a range of much warmer feelings in Helen and me for each other. Previously, periods of negative transferences had been interspersed with feelings of intense love in a totalistic, overstimulating form. Now there were stretches of loving feelings that had a much more personal, less overwhelming quality. It was as if Helen could actually begin to see me as a real person, and I found myself feeling a deep fondness for her, interspersed with occasional erotic interest. I realized that there had been something in the always explosive atmosphere of the transference-countertransference that had made it too dangerous for either of us to sustain intensely positive feelings for long. Crucial work with hatred needed to be accomplished before our relationship became safe enough for warmer feelings. Nevertheless, the fear of being hatefully coerced remained as long as we worked together, operating like a psychic trapdoor through which all other, more positive feelings and experiences could suddenly and totally disappear.

With Ben, a social interest lawyer with whom I had worked for years with considerably constructive results, we returned again and again to his deep fear that I would be unable to help him with the depths of his depression. His childhood had been organized around his mother's debilitating depression, and he longed for me to save him from despair more successfully than he had been able to save his mother from hers. Whatever positive developments we had been able to accomplish were episodically obliterated, because he was still sometimes depressed and my analytic efforts had not purged him of that potential. Six or seven years into the work, I found myself having two outbursts of hateful exasperation toward him. At one point I told him that, if I were him and felt the way he does, as boxed in and trapped, I would be taking antidepressants. At another point I pretty much blurted out that I felt we had come as far as we could go analytically. I believed, I told him, that he was continuing analysis at this point because he longed for me magically to save him. And that longing, although very understandable in terms of his life, was trapping him rather than facilitating a process that could help him any further. He maintained his complex, partly passive-aggressive longing by always maintaining that the analysis should "go deeper." "This is as deep as it gets," I said.

I believe that the content of what I said at both points had some merit. Antidepressants are a complex option for many patients, and my interpretation of the magical feature of his transference longings was something he and I had spoken about at various times before. But I brought up both issues at that point because I had reached the end of my rope, and that was pretty clear to both of us. In hindsight, we might say that Ben and I were struggling, in the dense interactive field that constituted our relationship, with problems of affect and boundaries within each of us and between us.

There were important resonances in the ways in which Ben and I were put together: both of us struggled with certain depressive affects; both of us pursued lives organized, to some extent, around counterdepressive defenses involved with helping others. Ben's depressive affect sometimes evoked (Mode 2) depressive feelings in me, which I tended to deal with by redoubling my efforts at staying with his feelings and working with him. But there were ways in which Ben's depression, through identification with his mother, had become a way of life; intense devotion to a depressed other had come to be experienced as the deepest form of love and attachment. So, in different sectors of his life, Ben played out (Mode 3) roles of the hopelessly depressed and the steadfast savior, and we played out these roles together in our relationship as well.

Ben was quite upset at these outbursts of mine, and we spent a long time processing them. One way he described his initial upset was to say that he felt as if he had been hit in the stomach with a shovel. We were both struck by the specificity of the image of the shovel; his association was to a spade. "Maybe I felt you were finally calling a spade a spade," he suggested. We continued to struggle (Mode 4) for a long time about the different meaning to each of us of my outbursts. For him, "This is as deep as it gets" meant I wanted at that moment to end his treatment. For me, "This is as keep as it gets" meant that this issue is the one we need to resolve; there are no others more important. But the struggle itself around these different meanings, probably both operative, proved fruitful.

I don't believe I would have allowed myself to express my exasperation so openly with Ben if we hadn't had a long history together, which gave me some confidence that we would be able to deal with it. In fact, we were. It subsequently became clear that there was something in my exasperation that suggested a limit to how much responsibility I was willing to bear for his depression, the kind of limit he was never able to set with his mother in her claims on him.

Very important developments emerged in the months following these transference-countertransference struggles. Two moments were particularly memorable and amusing. Ben came into one session quite uncharacteristically joyful. He'd been reading *Snow White* to his young son, and it struck him that it was in some sense the story of his own life. He often experienced his wife as a woman of great richness and depth. Yet, through the filter of his depressive episodes, he not infrequently lost these qualities in her, which had led him to marry her in the first place, and instead saw her as dull, chaotic, and humdrum. He would disparage her and compare her unfavorably to other women who appeared exciting from a distance. But the fairy tale put him in touch with a kind of radiant simplicity in his wife that took on a new meaning to him.

The domestic warmth that Snow White brought to the dreary life of the dwarfs seemed emblematic of some of the domestic and romantic satisfactions his wife provided him and from which he was generally distracted by his misery. It also occurred to him that he was the dwarfs. He saw himself in Doc, Sleepy, Sneezy, and especially in Grumpy, but he wasn't just the dwarfs; he was also the Prince. This session initiated a greater capacity than he previously had felt to contain a multiplicitous experience of his various qualities: passivity, irritability, an allergic hypersensitivity (like Sneezy), an aristocratic sense of entitlement, and a genuinely, uniquely radiant intelligence and capacity to connect deeply to others.

In another session around the same time, Ben explored the similarities between me and an interior decorator he and his wife had been using enthusiastically. His company was called "Use What You Own" and offered consultations on improving one's decor, at a cost that was something short of the customary king's ransom, by rearranging some of the owner's current possessions. We kidded about my stance toward him in the analysis as a "Use What You Own" approach. Previously, he felt I was offering him a dwarflike dreary maturity (slaving away in the mines) while he was holding out for a happy ending (in the castle) that would surely be his, if he just stayed in analysis long enough. Now he began to feel that the longings he had constructed in his childhood to keep hope alive in a truly dreadful and dreary world had become obstacles to his experiencing a kind of robustness and vitality in what his present life provided. With Ben as with Helen, there seemed to be something about the sorting out of hatred and exasperation, and the establishment of boundaries of responsibility, that opened up possibilities of other kinds of experience, more playful and appreciative.

Case histories in the psychoanalytic literature almost always have happy endings; I don't want to end this book with the impression that love and hate have always gone well between me and my patients. There have been patients I lost because either my love or my hate for them—sometimes both, I came to realize after their departure — were not clear enough to me, or were too intense for me, to be able to find a way to use them constructively. I am also sure there have been other patients who have left in mutually unsatisfying terminations in which loves and hates I never became aware of played an important part.

I *would* like to conclude by stressing that we are at the point in thinking about complex emotions in the analytic relationship where we can move beyond polarized positions about analytic love as either real or unreal, and analytic feelings as to be either carefully restrained or loosely expressed. Love and hate within the analytic relationship are very real, but are also contextual. The asymmetrical structure of the analytic situation is a powerful shaper of the feelings that emerge within it, making certain kinds of feelings possible and precluding others. It is precisely because these feelings, as real as they are, are so context-dependent that they are not easily translatable into extra- or postanalysis relationships. And neither restraint nor expressiveness, in themselves, are useful as guides to the management of analytic feelings. Both restraint and spontaneity can be either thoughtful or thoughtless. It is a central feature of the analyst's craft to struggle with these distinctions, to make what seems to be the best choices at the time, and continually to reconsider past judgments and their sequelae, in order to expand and enrich the context in which current choices are made.

ENDNOTES

PREFACE

1. Orbach (1998) has noted that our bodies are just as culturally shaped and constructed as our minds.

2. Cooper (1988) has suggested that Loewald's use of traditional terms whose meanings he has subtly changed has resulted in a broad acceptance of his work by people who do not really understand him.

CHAPTER 1

1. Loewald's vision of a primal density has interesting implications for the controversy generated by Daniel Stern's (1985) critique of Mahler's concept of an early symbiotic phase of development. The child's experience, Stern argued, is not undifferentiated, as Mahler has suggested, but organized from the beginning around distinctions between internal and external, self and others. Unlike Mahler, Loewald believed that a primary, undifferentiated mode of organization is not simply a distinct early phase, but is coterminous with more complex organizations throughout life. Therefore, for Loewald, primary density does not imply, as it does for Mahler, experience that is primitive or undeveloped. Unlike Stern, Loewald believed that despite impressive cognitive capacities the infant (or the adult) might possess, experience is organized throughout life in both differentiated and undifferentiated modes. These distinctions are filled out in this and the following chapter.

2. It should be noted that many contemporary philosophers of language, following Wittgenstein, would have problems with Stern's (1985) distinction between experience "as it is lived and as it is verbally represented," because lived experience is understood to take place only in semiotic, linguistic terms.

3. Loewald grounds his own views, as he generally does, in a subtext of Freud's, in this case an undeveloped hint of an earlier correspondence between the "thing" and the "word," which, puzzlingly, seems to predate the distinction between unconscious and preconscious (Loewald, 1977a, pp. 181–183).

4. Some features of Loewald's view of language in primary process experience (and Stern's view of early preverbal experience) were anticipated by Schachtel (1959) in his remarkable book *Metamorphosis*. Schactel argued that infantile amnesia for early childhood experience is caused not, as Freud believed, by a repression of infantile sexuality, but by a sharp discontinuity in the organizing patterns through which early and later modes of experience are processed. Early theorizing about psychedelic drugs (e.g., Aldous Huxley's *The Doors of Perception* [1970], for whom the rock group "The Doors" was named) speculated that powerful hallucinogens like mescalin and LSD undercut developmentally later forms of organizing experience and revitalize experience as it appears in the earliest months of life.

5. The deadening of language is probably an inevitable feature of its overuse, in which the original freshness of a formulation or understanding is dulled in its repetition. But the deadening of psychoanalytic language has also been partly a function of active editorial policies on the part of its journals. Innovative thinking is regularly shoehorned into a format in which new ideas are presented as already discoverable in Freud, either explicitly or implicitly. By the time the reader has reached the ideas themselves, her senses have been dulled into a disbelief in the very possibility of fresh thought.

6. See Sands (1997), Crastnopol (1997), and Stolorow, Atwood, and Orange (1998) for an informative debate on the implications of the concept and the term "projective identification."

7. Steiner (1978) characterizes Heidegger's methodology, which he terms "the cardinal move in Heideggerian philosophy," as follows:

One takes a common locution, or a passage in Heraclitus, in Kant, in Nietzsche. One excavates from individual syllables, words, or phrases their original, long-buried, or eroded wealth of meaning. One demonstrates that the occlusion of this meaning has altered and damaged the destiny of Western thought, and how its rediscovery, its literal restoration to active radiance, can bring on a renascence of intellectual and moral possibility [p. 8].

By substituting Freud for the other authors, this could stand as a very apt characterization of Loewald's methodology.

8. The capacity of language, in poetry and in psychoanalysis, to generate and transform states of mind is a major theme of Ogden's (1999) remarkable *Reverie and Interpretation.*

9. Recent studies of bilingualism (Perez Foster, 1996) in analytic treatment have highlighted the ways in which the sounds of particular words in a particular language evoke total states of mind (and, often, accompanying memories) that do not lend themselves to translation.

10. Thus, in Hartmann's distinction in the ego's realms between a conflictual and a confict-free (primary autonomous) sphere, the ego was divided into one portion still representing the id, primarily defensive and at odds with reality, and another portion, wired to be adapted to and to join forces with reality. It should be noted that many European Freudians (particularly the French) regard this ego-psychological extension of the powers of the ego vis-à-vis the id as a betrayal of Freud's vision. For them, the id-ego and social reality are no less intrinsically at odds, but their sympathies lie more on the side of the instincts (defined in terms of the more appealing *desire,* rather than the American term *impulse*) over and against conventional social reality.

11. Again it is possible to trace the influence of Heidegger's depictions of being as inseparable from "Being-in-the world," on Loewald's understanding of the relationship of the psyche to social reality.

It is not the case that man "is" and then has, by way of an extra, a relationship-of-being toward the "world" — a world with which he provides himself occasionally. *Dasein* is never "proximally" an entity which is, so to speak, free from Being-in, but which sometimes has the inclination to take up a "relationship" toward the world [Steiner, 1978, p. 84].

12. One could read Winnicott here as not meaning "illusion" in a literal sense, but something more fanciful and paradoxical, more like the imagistic in art, which doesn't suggest an antithesis to "reality" (E. Ghent, personal communication).

13. I am indebted to Judith Brisman, who told me about this case.

14. The Columbian surrealist author Gabriel García Márquez has always insisted that the magical flights that take place in *One Hundred Years of Solitude* came not from his imagination, but from the running stories told him by his grandparents during his childhood, at an age when he could make no distinction between fact and legend, or between rumor and reality (Reid, 1997).

15. Scattered throughout Loewald's writings, from his earliest papers to his final book, *Sublimation,* are suggestions, always undeveloped, of his deep critique of traditional psychoanalytic epistemology.

> I believe it to be necessary and timely to question that assumption, handed to us from the nineteenth century, that the scientific approach to the world and the self represents a higher and more mature evolutionary stage of man than the religious way of life. But I cannot pursue this question here [Loewald, 1960, p. 228].

16. Castoriadis (1991) has criticized both Freud and American Freudian ego psychology along very similar lines. He suggests that Freud's use of the reclamation of the Zuider Zee to illustrate the progressive analytic conquest of the id by the ego is fundamentally misconceived.

> The unconscious is implicitly presented there as a sort of dirty, stagnant water which you have to reclaim, to dry up and to

cultivate. Well, I think this is both unrealistic, utopian and wrong . . . the traditional idea seems to be to clear up the unconscious, to close this chapter and to have the subject, the patient, living happily ever after with a strong ego. This has been the classical American tendency and the American meaning of "autonomy." I think this is wrong because the true nucleus of the individual's radical imagination is rooted in the unconscious . . . we never reclaim the contents of the id. You change the relationship between the two agencies, that's all [p. 489].

CHAPTER 2

1. As he notes in an important paper, "On Internalization" (1973),

I cannot in this paper discuss the assumption of primary ego autonomy [Hartmann], which is not in keeping with the ideas on ego formation advanced here. In my opinion Hartmann's hypothesis raises metapsychological problems, which render its unquestioned acceptance premature, to say the least [p. 81].

2. Freud and some subsequent theorists (e.g., Edith Jacobson, 1964) also wrote about "primary identifications" in which the boundary between self and object was blurred. But these also were understood as discrete phenomena.

3. This approach to the relationship between memory and perception has interesting resonance with the notion of "re-entrant loops," central to Gerald Edelman's (1992) influential Neural Darwinism theory of mind.

4. The connection between Loewald's work and Bion's around the concept of "linking" is evocative.

5. Loewald (1977b) writes,

I wish now to stress the risks of misunderstanding and distortion when the analytic situation is compared with the early parent-child dyadic relationship, as illuminating as this comparison is in many respects. When all is said and done . . . analysis . . . is a venture in which the analysand not only is chronologically a grown-up, but that makes sense only if his or her adult potential, as manifested in certain significant areas of life, is in evidence [p. 380].

6. A frequently cited passage in the work of Racker (1968) emphasizing the symmetry between analysand and analyst might serve as a counterpoint to the asymmetry highlighted by Loewald's parent-child model.

The first distortion of truth in "the myth of the analytic situation" is that analysis is an interaction between a sick person and a healthy one. The truth is that it is an interaction between two personalities, in both of which the ego is under pressure from the id, the superego, and the external world; each personality has its internal and external dependencies, anxieties, and pathological defenses; each is also a child with his internal parents; and each of these whole personalities — that of the analysand and that of the analyst — responds to every event in the analytic situation [p. 132].

7. At another point, Loewald (1978a) suggests that "The richer a person's mental life is, the more he experiences on several levels of mentation, the more translation occurs back and forth between unconscious and conscious experience. To make the unconscious conscious, is one-sided. It is the *transference* between them that makes a human life, that makes life human" (p. 31).

CHAPTER 3

1. Other authors have also employed hierarchical schemes as an organizational framework for distinguishing different features of mind. See, for example, Gedo and Goldberg (1973) and Wilson and Gedo (1998). The way in which Loewald and Ogden established their

hierarchical organizational levels are particularly suited to comparing and contrasting different relational perspectives.

2. In her "Event Theory," Irene Fast (1980) has developed a very rich and useful process-oriented systems approach that also incorporates transpersonal affective dimensions, which I have heuristically separated out and designated Mode 2.

3. For an insightful comparative study of various concepts of subjectivity and intersubjectivity, see Teicholz (1998).

4. There have been recent, very important explorations of the role of seduction in the psychoanalytic relationship (see Davies and Frawley, 1994; Davies, 1999; Maroda, 1999).

CHAPTER 4

1. In Bowlby's relationship with ethology, influence worked in both directions. Bowlby picked up the concept of "imprinting" from ethology, and it became an important underpinning of his theory of attachment. But Bowlby influenced ethologists as well. In his research on children, Bowlby became impressed with the enormous impact of separation on the young, and ethologists like Hinde and Harlow both developed separation into an important area of ethological research because of Bowlby's impact on their work (John Kerr, personal communication).

2. Among Bowlby's last works (1990) was a biography of Darwin. See Sulloway (1996, pp. 140–145) for an interesting discussion of Darwin's impact on Bowlby.

3. John Kerr (personal communication) notes that the analytic situation might be construed very usefully as a version of the "strange situation" and the patient's approach to the analyst as a variation on the reunion with the mother (through the transference) following her return in the "strange situation." Connie's initial

structuring of distance in the analytic relationship to me might well be considered a kind of avoidant attachment style.

CHAPTER 5

1. Fairbairn's concept of "object-seeking" as an essential feature of human nature seems somewhat crude to the modern ear, ascribing to the neonate a fairly complex motivational system. In recent years, the study of what processes are built into the human organism and the ways in which they become organized over the course of development, through interaction, have become much more sophisticated. For example, Ghent (in press), drawing on Edelman's "neural Darwinism" and nonlinear dynamic systems theories, suggests that it is more conceptually rigorous to speak of primitive biases or values built into the human fetus which, under conditions of normative environment, evolve into what secondarily become motivational systems, e.g., the need for attachment to objects.

CHAPTER 6

1. See Stepansky (1999) for a fascinating exploration of Freud's complex relationship to surgery and surgical metaphors.

2. For a critique of this trend in the relational literature, see Greenberg (in press). Greenberg sees the problem in the way in which clinical examples are presented. I regard the relational literature as much more thoughtful and balanced than he does, and see the problem as deriving more from a concretistic misreading of the literature, more for the purpose of direction than self-reflection (see the afterword in Mitchell, 1997). For responses to Greenberg's critique, see Crastnopol (in press) and Pizer (in press).

3. The relational literature of the past decades is full of carefully considered clinical examples in which examples of expressiveness are weighed and balanced against considerations of restraint. Many examples could be cited, including: Aron (1996), Bromberg (1998),

Hoffman (1998), Maroda (1991, 1999), Mitchell (1993, 1997), Pizer (1998), Slochower (1996). For a particularly thoughtful exchange on these issues, see Davies (1998) and accompanying commentaries: Cooper (1998), Gabbard (1998), and Hoffman (1998b).

4. Hoffman (1998b) points out that even though we encourage patients, in one way or another, to express what is on their mind, we count on them to use discretion and tact in the forms of expression as a precondition for constructive psychoanalytic dialogue.

5. My choice to raise the issues of literal limits and boundaries at that point undoubtedly had many motivational currents in the transference and countertransference. Was my timing partly a reflection of my own anxieties? Was I responding to a cueing by Gloria about what had become less useful to her? Our discrete roles in the interactions that led to this turn are ultimately inextricable from each other; however, it seems crucial to me to keep asking these questions.

REFERENCES

Altman, N. (1995), *The Analyst in the Inner City: Race, Class and Culture Through a Psychoanalytic Lens*. Hillsdale, NJ: The Analytic Press.

Arlow, J. & Brenner, C. (1964), *Psychoanalytic Concepts and the Structural Theory*. New York: International Universities Press.

Aron, L. (1996), *A Meeting of Minds: Mutuality in Psychoanalysis*. Hillsdale, NJ: The Analytic Press.

Bass, A. (1996), Holding, holding back, and holding on. *Psychoanal. Dial.*, 6:361–378.

Beebe, B., Lachmann, F. & Jaffe, J. (1997), Mother–infant interaction structures and presymbolic self and object representations. *Psychoanal. Dial.*, 7:133–182.

Benjamin, J. (1988), *The Bonds of Love: Psychoanalysis, Feminism, and the Problem of Domination*. New York: Pantheon.

———— (1995), *Like Subjects, Love Objects*. New Haven, CT: Yale University Press.

———— (1998), *The Shadow of the Other: Intersubjectivity and Gender in Psychoanalysis*. New York: Routledge.

Black, M. (in press), Rethinking change: Enactment as the medium or the message. *Psychoanal. Dial.*

Bowlby, J. (1960), Grief and mourning in infancy and early childhood. *The Psychoanalytic Study of the Child*, 15:9–52. New York: International Universities Press.

———— (1969), *Attachment and Loss, Vol. 1 – Attachment*. New York: Basic Books.

———— (1973), *Attachment and Loss, Vol. 2 – Separation: Anxiety and Anger*. New York: Basic Books.

———— (1980), *Attachment and Loss, Vol. 3 – Loss: Sadness and Depression*. New York: Basic Books.

———— (1990), *Charles Darwin: A New Life*. New York: Norton.

Bromberg, P. M. (1998), *Standing in the Spaces: Essays on Clinical Process, Trauma, and Dissociation.* Hillsdale, NJ: The Analytic Press.

Burke, W. (1992), Countertransference disclosure and the asymmetry/mutuality dilemma. *Psychoanal. Dial.,* 2:241–271.

Cavell, M. (1993), *The Psychoanalytic Mind: From Freud to Philosophy.* Cambridge, MA: Harvard University Press.

Castoriadis, C. (1991), Interview with Paul Gordon. *Free Associations,* 2:483–506.

Chodorow, N. (1999), *The Power of Feelings: Personal Meaning in Psychoanalysis, Gender and Culture.* New Haven, CT: Yale University Press.

Cooper, A. (1988), Our changing views of the therapeutic action of psychoanalysis: Comparing Strachey and Loewald. *Psychoanal. Quart.,* 57:15–27.

Cooper, S. (1998), Flirting, post-Oedipus, and mutual protectiveness in the analytic dyad. *Psychoanal. Dial.,* 8:767–780.

Crastnopol, M. (1997), When does a theory stop being itself? *Psychoanal. Dial.,* 7:683–690.

_____ (in press), On the need for a different kind of "book." *J. Amer. Psychoanal. Assn.*

Davies, J. M. (1996), Linking the pre-analytic with the postclassical: Integration, dissociation, and the multiplicity of unconscious process. *Contemp. Psychoanal.,* 32:553–576.

_____ (1998a), Between the disclosure and foreclosure of erotic transference-countertransference: Can psychoanalysis find a place for adult sexuality? *Psychoanal. Dial.,* 8:747–766.

_____ (1998b), The multiple aspects of multiplicity: Symposium on clinical choices in psychoanalysis. *Psychoanal. Dial.,* 8:195–206.

_____ & Frawley, M. G. (1994), *Treating the Adult Survivor of Childhood Sexual Abuse: A Psychoanalytic Perspective.* New York: Basic Books.

DeCasper, A. & Fifer, W. (1980), Of human bonding: Newborns prefer their mothers' voices. *Science,* 208:1174–1176.

Demos, V. (1999), The search for psychological models. *Psychoanal. Dial.*, 9:219–227.

Eagle, M. (1993), Why do we need objects? Presented at Invited Panel Division 39, American Psychological Assn., New York City, April 17.

Edelman, G. (1992), *Bright Air, Brilliant Fire: On the Matter of the Mind.* New York: Basic Books.

Eigen, M. (1981), The area of faith in Winnicott, Lacan and Bion. *Internat. J. Psycho-Anal.*, 62:413–433.

Fairbairn, W. R. D. (1952), *An Object Relations Theory of the Personality.* New York: Basic Books.

———— (1954), Observations on the nature of hysterical states. In: *From Instinct to Self: Selected Papers of W. R. D. Fairbairn*, ed. D. Scharff & E. Birtles. New York: Aronson, 1994, pp. 13–40.

Farber, L. (1976), *Lying, Despair, Jealousy, Envy, Sex, Suicide, Drugs, and the Good Life.* New York: Basic Books.

———— (1999), Will and anxiety. *Salmagundi*, 123:141–160.

Fast, I. (1985), *Event Theory: A Piaget–Freud Integration.* Hillsdale, NJ: The Analytic Press.

Fonagy, P., Moran, G. S., Steele, M. & Steele, H. (1992), The integration of psychoanalytic theory and work on attachment: The issue of intergenerational psychic processes. In: *Attaccamento e Psicoanalisis*, ed. D. Stern & M. Ammaniti. Bari, Italy: Laterzo, pp. 19–30.

———— Steele, M., Steele, H., Leigh, T., Kennedy, R., Mattoon, G. & Target, M. (1995), Attachment, the reflective self, and borderline states: The predictive specificity of the Adult Attachment Interview and pathological emotional development. In: *Attachment Theory*, ed. S. Goldberg, R. Muir & J. Kerr. Hillsdale, NJ: The Analytic Press.

———— & Target, M. (1996), Playing with reality I: Theory of mind and the normal development of psychic reality. *Internat. J. Psycho-Anal.*, 77:217–233.

———— & ———— (1998), Mentalization and the changing aims of child psychoanalysis. *Psychoanal. Dial.*, 8:87–114.

Frank, K. (1999), *Psychoanalytic Participation: Action, Interaction, and Integration.* Hillsdale, NJ: The Analytic Press.

Freud, S. (1913), Totem and taboo. *Standard Edition,* 13:1–162. London: Hogarth Press, 1955.

_____ (1917), Mourning and melancholia. *Standard Edition,* 14:248–258. London: Hogarth Press, 1957.

_____ (1920), Beyond the pleasure principle. *Standard Edition,* 18:3–64. London: Hogarth Press, 1955.

_____ (1921), Group psychology and the analysis of the ego. *Standard Edition,* 18:67–143. London: Hogarth Press, 1955.

_____ (1923), The ego and the id. *Standard Edition,* 19:3–66. London: Hogarth Press, 1961.

_____ (1924), The dissolution of the Oedipus complex. *Standard Edition,* 19:173–179. London: Hogarth Press, 1961.

_____ (1930), Civilization and its discontents. *Standard Edition,* 21:64–145. London: Hogarth Press, 1961.

_____ (1940), Outline of psychoanalysis. *Standard Edition,* 23:139–207. London: Hogarth Press, 1964.

Fromm, E. (1956), *The Art of Loving.* New York: Harper.

_____ (1994), *The Art of Listening.* New York: Continuum.

Fromm-Reichmann, F. (1950), *Principles of Intensive Psychotherapy.* Chicago: University of Chicago Press.

Gabbard, G. (1996), *Love and Hate in the Analytic Setting.* Northvale, NJ: Aronson.

_____ (1998), Commentary on paper by Jody Messler Davies. *Psychoanal. Dial.,* 8:781–790.

Gedo, J. & Goldberg, A. (1973), *Models of the Mind.* Chicago: University of Chicago Press.

Ghent, E. (1992), Process and paradox. *Psychoanal. Dial.,* 2:135–159.

_____ (in press), Wish, need, drive, motive in the light of dynamic systems theory. *Psychoanal. Dial.*

Gill, M. (1994), *Psychoanalysis in Transition.* Hillsdale, NJ: The Analytic Press.

Goldberg, S., Muir, R. & Kerr, J. (1995), *Attachment Theory: Social, Developmental, and Clinical Perspectives.* Hillsdale, NJ: The Analytic Press.

Goldman, D. (1996), *In Search of the Real: The Origins and Originality of D. W. Winnicott.* Northvale, NJ: Aronson.

Greenberg, J. (1991), *Oedipus and Beyond: A Clinical Theory.* Cambridge, MA: Harvard University Press.

————— (1996), A classic revisited: Loewald on the therapeutic action of psychoanalysis. *J. Amer. Psychoanal. Assn.,* 44:863–924.

————— (1999), Analytic authority and analytic restraint. *Contemp. Psychoanal.,* 35:25–42.

————— (in press), The analytic participation: A new look. *J. Amer. Psychoanal. Assn.*

Grotstein, J. (1981), *Splitting and Projective Identification.* New York: Aronson.

————— (1990), Introduction. In: *Psychotic Anxieties and Containment* by M. Little. Northvale, NJ: Aronson.

Habermas, J. (1968), *Knowledge and Human Interests.* New York: Beacon.

Havens, L. (1997), A linguistic contribution to psychoanalysis. *Psychoanal. Dial.,* 7:523–534.

Hirsch, I. (1998), Further thoughts about interpersonal and relational perspectives. *Contemp. Psychoanal.,* 34:501–538.

Hoffman, I. Z. (1998a), *Ritual and Spontaneity in the Psychoanalytic Process.* Hillsdale, NJ: The Analytic Press.

————— (1998b), Poetic transformations of erotic experience. *Psychoanal. Dial.,* 8:791–804.

Holmes, J. (1996), *Attachment, Intimacy, Autonomy.* Northvale, NJ: Aronson.

Hunter, V. (1991), John Bowlby: An interview. *Psychoanal. Rev.,* 78:159–175.

Huxley, A. (1970), *The Doors of Perception.* New York: Harper & Row.

Jacobs, T. (1991), *The Use of the Self.* New York: International Universities Press.

Jacobson, E. (1964), *The Self and the Object World.* New York: International Universities Press.

Kernberg, O. (1980), *Internal World and External Reality.* New York: Aronson.

Klein, M. (1975), *Envy and Gratitude and Other Works, 1946–1963*. New York: Delacorte Press.

Kumin, I. (1996), *Pre-Object Relatedness: Early Attachment and the Psychoanalytic Situation*. New York: Guilford Press.

Lear, J. (1990), *Love and Its Place in Nature: A Philosophical Interpretation of Freudian Analysis*. New York: Farrar, Straus & Giroux.

_____ (1998), *Open-Minded: Working Out the Logic of the Soul*. Cambridge, MA: Harvard University Press.

Levenson, E. (1972), *The Fallacy of Understanding: An Inquiry into the Changing Structure of Psychoanalysis*. New York: Basic Books.

_____ (1983), *The Ambiguity of Change: An Inquiry into the Nature of Psychoanalytic Reality*. New York: Basic Books.

Lionells, M., Fiscalini, J., Mann, C. & Stern, D. (1995), *Handbook of Interpersonal Psychoanalysis*. Hillsdale, NJ: The Analytic Press.

Loewald, H. (1949), The ego and reality. In: *Papers on Psychoanalysis*. New Haven, CT: Yale University Press, 1980, pp. 3–20.

_____ (1951), The problem of defense and the neurotic interpretation of reality. In: *Papers on Psychoanalysis*. New Haven, CT: Yale University Press, 1980, pp. 21–32.

_____ (1960), On the therapeutic action of psychoanalysis. In: *Papers on Psychoanalysis*. New Haven, CT: Yale University Press, 1980, pp. 221–256.

_____ (1965), On internalization. In: *Papers on Psychoanalysis*. New Haven, CT: Yale University Press, 1980, pp. 69–86.

_____ (1966), Book review: *Psychoanalytic Concepts and the Structural Theory* by Jacob A. Arlow & Charles Brenner. In: *Papers on Psychoanalysis*. New Haven, CT: Yale University Press, 1980, pp. 53–68.

_____ (1970), Psychoanalytic theory and the psychoanalytic process. In: *Papers on Psychoanalysis*. New Haven, CT: Yale University Press, 1980, pp. 277–301.

_____ (1971a), On motivation and instinct theory. In: *Papers on Psychoanalysis*. New Haven, CT: Yale University Press, 1980, pp. 102–137.

_____ (1971b), The experience of time. In: *Papers on Psychoanalysis*. New Haven, CT: Yale University Press, 1980, pp. 138–147.

_____ (1972), Perspectives on memory. In: *Papers on Psychoanalysis*. New Haven, CT: Yale University Press, 1980, pp. 148–173.

_____ (1973), Book review: *The Analysis of the Self* by Heinz Kohut. In: *Papers on Psychoanalysis*. New Haven, CT: Yale University Press, 1980, pp. 342–351.

_____ (1974a), Psychoanalysis as an art and the fantasy character of the analytic situation. In: *Papers on Psychoanalysis*. New Haven, CT: Yale University Press, 1980, pp. 352–371.

_____ (1974b), Book review essay on the Freud/Jung Letters. In: *Papers on Psychoanalysis*. New Haven, CT: Yale University Press, 1980, pp. 405–418.

_____ (1977a), Primary process, secondary process and language. In: *Papers on Psychoanalysis*. New Haven, CT: Yale University Press, 1980, pp. 178–206.

_____ (1977b), Reflections on the psychoanalytic process and its therapeutic potential. In: *Papers on Psychoanalysis*. New Haven, CT: Yale University Press, 1980, pp. 372–383.

_____ (1978a), *Psychoanalysis and the History of the Individual*. New Haven, CT: Yale University Press.

_____ (1978b), The waning of the Oedipus complex. In: *Papers on Psychoanalysis*. New Haven, CT: Yale University Press, 1980.

_____ (1980), *Papers on Psychoanalysis*. New Haven, CT: Yale University Press.

_____ (1988), *Sublimation*. New Haven, CT: Yale University Press.

Mace, C. & Margison, R. (1997), Attachment and psychotherapy: An overview. *Brit. J. Med. Psychol.*, 70:209–215.

Main, M. (1995), Recent studies in attachment: Overview with selected implications for clinical social work. In: *Attachment Theory*, ed. S. Goldberg, R. Muir & J. Kerr. Hillsdale, NJ: The Analytic Press, pp. 407–474.

Maroda, K. (1991), *The Power of Countertransference*. Northvale, NJ: Aronson.

_____ (1999), *Seduction, Surrender, and Transformation*. Hillsdale, NJ: The Analytic Press.

McLaughlin, J. (1996), Loewald and the clinical work of psychoanalysis. *J. Amer. Psychoanal. Assn.*, 44:899–910.

Meltzer, D. (1975), Adhesive identification. *Contemp. Psychoanal.*, 11:289–310.

Milner, M. (1958), *On Not Being Able to Paint*. London: Heinemann.

Mitchell, S. (1988), The intrapsychic and the interpersonal: Different theories, different domains, or historical artifacts. *Psychoanal. Inq.*, 8:472–496.

_____ (1991), Contemporary pserspectives on self: Toward an integration. *Psychoanal. Dial.*, 1:121–147.

_____ (1993), *Hope and Dread in Psychoanalysis*. New York: Basic Books.

_____ (1997), *Influence and Autonomy in Psychoanalysis*. Hillsdale, NJ: The Analytic Press.

_____ & Aron, L. (1999), *Relational Psychoanalysis: The Emergence of a Tradition*. Hillsdale, NJ: The Analytic Press.

Muller, J. (1996), *Beyond the Psychoanalytic Dyad: Developmental Semiotics in Freud, Pierce and Lacan*. New York: Routledge.

Ogden, T. (1989), *The Primitive Edge of Experience*. Northvale, NJ: Aronson.

_____ (1997), *Reverie and Interpretation: Sensing Something Human*. Northvale, NJ: Aronson.

Orbach, S. (1998), Response to Stephen Mitchell. Conference of the Association for Attachment-Based Psychotherapy, London, February 17.

Perez Foster, R. (1996), The bilingual self. *Psychoanal. Dial.*, 6:99–122.

Phillips, A. (1995), *Terrors and Experts*. London: Faber & Faber.

Pine, F. (1990), *Drive, Ego, Object, Self.* New York: Basic Books.

Pinker, S. (1994), *The Language Instinct: How the Mind Creates Language*. New York: Morrow.

Pizer, S. (1998), *Building Bridges: The Negotiation of Paradox in Psychoanalysis*. Hillsdale, NJ: The Analytic Press.

_____ (in press), Looking for Greenberg: A commentary on his "new look."*J. Amer. Psychoanal. Assn.*

Racker, H. (1968), *Transference and Countertransference.* New York: International Universities Press.

Rapaport, D. (1958), The theory of ego autonomy: A generalization. In: *The Collected Papers of David Rapaport,* ed. M. Gill. New York: Basic Books, pp. 722–744.

Reid, A. (1997), Report from an undeclared war. *The New York Review of Books,* October 9, pp. 12–22.

Renik, O. (1996), The perils of neutrality. *Psychoanal. Quart.,* 65:495–517.

Rivera, J. (1989), Linking the psychological and the social: Feminism, post-structuralism and multiple personality. *Dissociation,* 2:24–31.

Sander, L. (in press), Thinking differently: Tasks and boundaries in constructing our pathway to the future. *Psychoanal. Dial.*

Sands, S. (1997), Self psychology and projective identification— Whither shall they meet? *Psychoanal. Dial.,* 7:651–668.

Schachtel, E. (1959), *Metamorphosis.* New York: Basic Books.

Schafer, R. (1968), *Aspects of Internalization.* New York: International Universities Press.

_____ (1976), *A New Language for Psychoanalysis.* New Haven, CT: Yale University Press.

_____ (1983), *The Analytic Attitude.* New York: Basic Books.

_____ (1992), *Retelling a Life: Narration and Dialogue in Psychoanalysis.* New York: Basic Books.

Scharff, D. & Birtles, E., eds. (1994), *From Instinct to Self: Selected Papers of W. R. D. Fairbairn.* Northvale, NJ: Aronson.

Seligman, S. (1999), Integrating Kleinian theory and intersubjective infant research observation. *Psychoanal. Dial.,* 9:129–159.

Skolnick, N. (1998), The good, the bad, and the ambivalent: Fairbairn's difficulty locating the good object in the endopsychic structure. In: *Fairbairn, Then and Now,* ed. N. Skolnick & D. Scharff. Hillsdale, NJ: The Analytic Press, pp. 137–159.

Slade, A. (1997), The implications of attachment theory and research for developmental theory and clinical process. Presented to Connecticut Society for Psychoanalytic Psychology, November 15.

_____ (1998), Attachment theory and research: Implications for the theory and practice of individual psychotherapy with adults. In: *The Handbook of Attachment Theory and Research*, ed. J. Cassidy & P. Shaver. New York: Guilford Press.

Slochower, J. (1996), *Holding and Psychoanalysis: A Relational Perspective*. Hillsdale, NJ: The Analytic Press.

Spezzano, C. (1993), *Affect in Psychoanalysis: A Clinical Synthesis*. Hillsdale, NJ: The Analytic Press.

Spillius, E. B. (1988), *Melanie Klein Today: Developments in Theory and Practice*, Vols. 1 & 2. London: Routledge.

Steiner, J. (1978), *Martin Heidegger*. Chicago: University of Chicago Press.

Stepansky, P. (1999), *Freud, Surgery, and the Surgeons*. Hillsdale, NJ: The Analytic Press.

Stern, D. B. (1997), *Unformulated Experience: From Dissociation to Imagination in Psychoanalysis*. Hillsdale, NJ: The Analytic Press.

Stern, D. N. (1985), *The Interpersonal World of the Infant*. New York: Basic Books.

_____ Sander, L., Nahum, J., Harrison, A., Lyons-Ruth, K., Moran, A., Bruschweiler-Stern, N. & Tronick, E. (1998), Noninterpretive mechanisms in psychoanalytic therapies: The "something more" than interpretation. *Internat. J. Psycho-Anal.*, 79:903–921.

Stolorow, R. & Atwood, G. (1992), *Contexts of Being: The Intersubjective Foundations of Psychological Life*. Hillsdale, NJ: The Analytic Press.

_____ _____ & Orange, D. (1998), Projective identification begone! *Psychoanal. Dial.*, 8:719–726.

_____ Brandchaft, G. & Atwood, G. (1987), *Psychoanalytic Treatment: An Intersubjective Approach*. Hillsdale, NJ: The Analytic Press.

Sullivan, H. S. (1950), The illusion of personal individuality. In: *The Fusion of Psychiatry and Social Science*. New York: Norton, 1964, pp. 198–226.

_____ (1953), *The Interpersonal Theory of Psychiatry.* New York: Norton.

_____ (1954), *The Psychiatric Interview.* New York: Norton.

Sulloway, F. (1996), *Born to Rebel.* New York: Vintage.

Suomi, S. (1995), Influence of attachment theory on ethological studies of biobehavioral development in nonhuman primates. In: *Attachment Theory,* ed. S. Goldberg, R. Muir & J. Kerr. Hillsdale, NJ: The Analytic Press, pp. 185–202.

Teicholz, J. (1998), *Kohut, Loewald, and the Postmoderns.* Hillsdale, NJ: The Analytic Press.

Trevarthen, C. & Hubley, P. (1978), Secondary intersubjectivity: Confidence, confiding and acts of meaning in the first year. In: *Action, Gesture and Symbol: The Emergence of Language,* ed. A. Lock. London: Academic Press.

Tronick, E., Als, H., Adamson, L., Wise, S. & Brazelton, T. B. (1978), The infant's response to entrapment between contradictory messages in face-to-face interaction. *J. Child Psychiat.,* 17:1–13.

van der Kolk, B. (1994), The body keeps the score: Approaches to the psychobiology of posttraumatic stress disorder. In: *Traumatic Stress,* ed. B. van der Kolk, A. McFarlane & L. Weisaeth. New York: Guilford Press, pp. 214–241.

White, M. (1977), Sullivan on treatment. *Contemp. Psychoanal.,* 13:317–346.

Wilson, A. & Gedo, J., eds. (1998), *Hierarchical Concepts in Psychoanalysis.* New York: Other Press.

Winnicott, D. W. (1960), Ego distortion in terms of true and false self. In: *The Maturational Processes and the Facilitating Environment.* New York: International Universities Press, 1965, pp. 140–152.

_____ (1971), The use of an object and relating through identifications. In: *Playing and Reality.* Harmondsworth, UK: Penguin, 1974.

_____ & Khan, M. (1953), A review of Fairbairn's *Psychoanalytic Studies of the Personality. Internat. J. Psycho-Anal.,* 34:329–333.

Yeats, W. B. (1933), *The Collected Poems of W. B. Yeats.* New York: Macmillan.

INDEX

seduction theory, ix, 84
  Freud's abandonment of, ix, x, 84
self- *vs.* field-regulatory processes, 57
self-disclosure, 126
self–other configurations (Mode 3),
  58, 62–67, 114, 123
  attachment and, 91–95, 115
  in case material, 72, 73, 75, 115,
    118, 120, 136, 141, 144
selfobjects, 63
Seligman, S., 69
sexual abuse. *See* George, case of sexual relations between analyst and
  patient, 133–134
sexuality, 113–115. *See also* love, and
  the erotic
Skolnick, N., 107
Slade, A., 82–83, 86
Slochower, J., 137
solipsism, xii
Spezzano, C., 68
Spillius, E. B., xiv
spontaneity in analytic interaction, 127,
  146
spontaneous gestures, 94, 95
Steele, H., 86
Steele, M., 86
Steiner, J., 12, 148n–150n
Stepansky, P., 154n
Stern, D. B., xv
Stern, D. N., 6–7, 60, 111, 147n
Stolorow, R., xv, 148n
"strange situation," 85, 153
structural theory, 32

sublimation, 18, 32, 150n
Sullivan, H. S., xv, 6, 7, 65, 95, 99, 101,
  105, 141
Sulloway, F., 153n
Suomi, S., 21
superego, "corruption" of, 120
surrender, 95, 114, 115, 128, 131, 132
symbiosis. *See also* boundaryless states;
  oceanic feeling
  and differentiation, 111–112
  mother–infant, 19
symbiotic phase of development,
  147n

Target, M., 86, 101
Teicholz, J., 153n
"third." *See* analytic third
time and memory, 45–47
transference, 24–25, 152n
Trevarthen, C., xv
Tronick, E., 62
"true self" experience, 94

union. *See* symbiosis

van der Kolk, B., 114

White, M., 65
will. *See* intentionality
Will, case of, 116–123
Wilson, A., 152n
Winnicott, D. W., 79, 95, 101, 107, 139
Wise, S., 62
Wittgenstein, Ludwig, 5